GRACE IS FOR YOU

Joel & Jenni,
Your calling & pilgrimage
are truely blessed w/
grace & peace.
   Thank you for becoming
a part of our life.

                    Herman Massey

GRACE IS FOR YOU

Flowing Like a River

HERMAN MASSEY

TATE PUBLISHING
AND **ENTERPRISES**, LLC

Published by Tate Publishing & Enterprises, LLC
127 E. Trade Center Terrace | Mustang, Oklahoma 73064 USA
1.888.361.9473 | www.tatepublishing.com

Tate Publishing is committed to excellence in the publishing industry. The company reflects the philosophy established by the founders, based on Psalm 68:11,
"The Lord gave the word and great was the company of those who published it."

Book design copyright © 2013 by Tate Publishing, LLC. All rights reserved.
Cover design by Jan Sunday Quilaquil
Interior design by Caypeeline Casas

Published in the United States of America

ISBN: 978-1-62510-449-6
1. Religion / Christian Life / General
2. Religion / Christian Life / Spiritual Growth
13.02.22

ACKNOWLEDGEMENTS

I want to thank my dear friend Merl Sholtess who read the first manuscript and made many valuable recommendations. Without his strong encouragement and positive input, this book would still be only in my computer.

I want to thank my brother Thurman Massey who read the manuscript and offered substantial recommendations related to the text. I also thank my brother Taylor Massey for his contributions to this work.

I also want to thank my wife Kathleen who tirelessly worked with me to edit and review the manuscript as it began to take shape. She spent many hours with me to improve the flow of the text

Finally, I want to thank Daryl and Kathy Shuck whose lives and ministry in grace inspired me to seek out the excellence of the knowledge of Christ Jesus my Lord in His administration of grace.

TABLE OF CONTENTS

INTRODUCTION

This book is the gleanings of a number of years of study and observation of many men and women of God. A wonderful group of these live and minister in the grace of God. Another wonderful group of them talk about grace but are still living under the law and trying to please God by human endeavor. This latter group is (in most cases) unaware of how restricting the law is and why there is so little evidence of the power, the peace, and the knowledge surpassing love of God flowing in their lives. I hope the following pages of this book will be a benefit to all of us in understanding the centrality of grace in our Heavenly Father's administration of His will.

This is not an academic or theological study of God's grace which has been poured out upon mankind. It is a humble attempt to describe what is not at all simple. What was in the nature of God—His infinite love, became manifested in the character of God. That is His grace. Think of it this way: God is love in His nature. When that love is demonstrated, it reveals God's character—God in action. It is precisely here that the operation of grace comes into view in God's relationship with His prize creation, man. We need no degree in philosophy or theology to participate to the fullest extent in God's grace. We joyfully may think of ourselves as Apostle Paul said of himself,

> *"To me, who am less than the least of all saints, was this grace given…."*

(Eph. 3:8)

If we asked most believers to define grace, they would say it is "God's unmerited favor." Indeed this is obviously and overwhelmingly true. That definition by itself (far reaching as it is) seems somewhat inadequate to meaningfully tell the whole story in the light of the New Testament's many verses revealing the operation of grace. The unfolding labor of the love of God has reached us through the person and work of Jesus Christ. This story is the central focus of the gospel of God. Both Luke and John open the record of Jesus as a child and as the Word of God with God's grace in full operation. Both speak of grace in His life. Here is the narrative:

> *"So when they had performed all things according to the law of the Lord, they returned to Galilee, to their own city, Nazareth. And the Child* [Jesus] *grew and became strong in spirit, filled with wisdom; and the grace of God was upon Him."*

(Luke 2:39-40)

Even with Jesus there was the need of grace from God his Father to be upon him. Why, you might wonder; it is because though Jesus was the son of God, he was fully man. And the Bible says that,

> *"It is written, 'Man shall not live by bread alone, but by every word that proceeds from the mouth of God.'"*

(Matt. 4:4)

This "*word*" from God was grace to the child Jesus.

When Jesus began to minister, John the apostle describes this "*word*" as animated in the person of Jesus the Word of God.

> *"And the Word became flesh and dwelt among us, and we beheld His glory, the glory as of the only begotten of the Father, full of grace and truth."*

(Jn. 1:14)

When one begins to explore the verses in the Bible wherein the word grace appears, he will find phrases that carry the mind over the top of analytical dimensions. Phrases like "the abundance of His grace," "the exceeding grace," "the exceeding riches of His grace," and "the manifold grace" truly reach the superlative levels of language. This divine vocabulary stretches our imagination when we read such phrases. Our pilgrim journey is then vaulted into heavenly arenas. That is where Christ is sitting at the right hand of God making intercession for us with human experience that now is not uniquely His own. Beloved, that human experience which is saturated with holiness, righteousness, faith, and overcoming victory is now intrinsically born into the life of every believer. It is God's gift to each believer; it is "*not of works*" (earned or deserved). Rather, it is grace!

Embracing this, I find it no mystery that the writers of the New Testament epistles would greet the beloved saints of God with, *"Grace to you from God our Father and the Lord Jesus Christ,"* and close with phrases like *"…grace be with you all."*

Indeed, we have found favor with God in our Lord and Savior Jesus Christ! Without question, it is unmerited, and I delightfully declare, it is unlimited! How could it be otherwise? God, our creator, who has created with purpose, has not abandoned the heartbeat of His ingenuity—man. The centrality of man in all God's creation is revealed in Zechariah 12:1. *"Thus says the Lord, who stretches out the heavens, lays the foundation of the earth, and forms the spirit of man within him."* This is carried to even greater heights in the apostle Paul's words:

> *"For we are His workmanship* [Gr. poiema— something made or done; it is transliterated into English as "poem"], *created in Christ Jesus for good works, which God prepared beforehand that we should walk in them."*

> (Eph. 2:10)

To the reader I would like to extend one small caveat from my heart. God's Word was given to His people as what seemed to Him the best means to provide for us a way to seek and find Him. It seems to me that people with the best of intentions have misunderstood this. Many have made the Bible something of a rule or guide book. Unfortunately, we find ourselves arguing over doctrines, measuring levels of presumed spiritual attainment, and judging one another's performance or lack thereof. Should we not rather embrace God's Word as the blessed facilitator to experience the richness of God in Christ with all of heaven's assets?

The misguided use of the Bible must sadden, perhaps even provoke our Father considerably. Let us lay self-examination and critiquing aside and look into the Bible as the pathway into our present life of divinely supplied human living. Let us fill our future destiny with eternal reward in an endless conscious presence of God. When the writer of Hebrews admonished us in chapter 12 that we were to lay aside every weight that so easily besets us, he may well have had in mind the law-making, law-keeping religion of man that tries to imitate godliness. Godliness cannot be counterfeited by human behavior. To think that we can be like God apart from God is a deception! The hundreds of years of Jewish history under the law consummated in a system in which Jesus identified religionists as children of the devil. (Do not misunderstand—I am not calling Jews "children of the devil." I am saying that Jesus said that the religious Pharisees were such.) Jesus came fulfilling the righteous requirement of the law. That is settled now. He said,

> *"I am the way, the truth, and the life; no one comes to the Father but by me."*

(Jn. 14:6)

Grace is about getting access to the Father to share the bounty of His resources! Jesus is the way to the availability of this grace.

To many Christians, the idea of Christ being our life seems mysterious. However, that is exactly the gospel of the New Testament. The Bible clearly tells us that Jesus came to give us life—His life. That life is uniquely what can please God. Isn't it time for us to quit making excuses for our failure to live in what this gospel speaks to us by trying to explain away many of the realities of the Biblical message? When we realize the supernatural function of grace that comes through Jesus, we will be able to lay aside all our excuses about being less than victorious Christians. Why shall we not simply embrace its message of grace with thankful hearts and joyful expectation? With this revelation we can embrace the simple message of grace and allow the operation of grace to perform in us what God is looking for in His people. Jesus did not come to judge us or condemn us. He came to save us and set us free by delivering us from our sins and releasing our benevolent Father's rivers of grace.

Regarding the verses on grace that will follow, I feel compelled to make the following statement. I understand and highly regard contextual integrity. However, I am seriously concerned that we have overachieved in systematic theology and thus elevated the mind over the Spirit. Consequently, the church has fallen far short of her mission to disciple the nations in the authority, power and ascendancy of Jesus the Christ. In this matter, I have sought a significant change in my own mind with the hope to become a disciple in the true New Testament sense.

The more I learn of the excellence of Christ, the more I am overwhelmed with the realization of how incomprehensively vast He is. Like Paul, I too rejoice saying,

> *"Oh the depth of the riches of the wisdom and knowledge of God! How unsearchable are His judgments and untraceable are His ways! For who has known the mind of the Lord, or who has been His counselor?"*

(Rom. 11:33-34)

Paul identifies the expansiveness of who Christ is in his prayer for the saints in Ephesus. He said,

> *"That you, being rooted and grounded in love, may be able to comprehend* [lay hold of] *with all the saints what is the width and length and depth and height—to know the love of Christ which passes knowledge; that you may be filled with all the fullness of God."*

(Eph. 3:17-19)

My fellow believers in Christ, I want to be filled up with Christ! I am confident that you do too!

Consider Paul's words regarding grace in Romans 4:16,

> *"Therefore it is of faith that it might be according to grace, so that the promise might be sure to all the seed, not only to those who are of the*

law, but also to those who are of the faith of Abraham, who is the father of us all."

In chapter 4, Paul is laying the firm foundation of the normal Christian life by affirming that it is not by the effort or righteousness of our striving that our relationship with God is secured. Rather, it is exclusively by faith in what God has accomplished in Jesus. Notice *"faith"* is *"according to grace."* It is not the other way around! It seems that the word *"according to"* implies the nature, availability, and accessibility of God's grace. This grace is the whole sphere in which God has worked effectively to accomplish salvation for us. It personifies all the saving work that has been accomplished for us by Jesus Christ.

The outcome of faith according to grace follows:

> *"so that the promise might be sure* [accessible, reliable and sound] *to all the seed."*

> (Rom. 4:16)

Then in Romans 5:1-2, Paul reiterates and validates this reality.

> *"Therefore, having been justified by faith, we have peace with God through our Lord Jesus Christ, through whom also we have access by faith into this grace in which we stand, and rejoice in hope of the glory of God."*

Think about what he has said here. It is the gospel, the heavenly proclamation from God through Paul.

"We have been justified by faith; we have peace with God; we also have access by faith into this grace, in which we stand!" The resource that faith is moving the believers into is God's grace. That makes me want to shout, and rejoice with joy and praise! This is *"Christ in me the hope of glory."* (Col. 1:27) Such a glory is not just objectively God's. This glory has subjectively enveloped you and me as the sons of God—the objects of His love, mercy, and labor in the salvation that is in Jesus! Are you shouting yet?

I submit the content of these pages to the Lord for His anointing. I submit it to you for your encouragement and strengthening as you are led on your own life journey by the Holy Spirit. Please read it with expectation! The *"God of all grace"* is with you! He gave us a small foretaste of the "coming grace" through Jeremiah the prophet saying,

> *"For I know the thoughts that I think toward you, says the* LORD, *thoughts of peace and not of evil, to give you a future and a hope. Then you will call upon Me and go and pray to Me, and I will listen to you. And you will seek Me and find Me, when you search for Me with all your heart. I will be found by you, says the* LORD.*"*

(Jer. 29:11-14)

I want to specifically emphasize and reemphasize that grace is a gift that God gives you! Throughout the book, this is the main theme. Nothing we do earns us even a smidgen of grace. Please, let the Holy Spirit write this indelibly into your heart and mind. Never think otherwise. Don't let the enemy of God (Satan) deceive you into trying to do something, anything—thinking that somehow you will gain a little favor, thus putting God in an obligatory position of debt to you. No, no, NO!

CHAPTER 1

THE MANIFOLD GRACE OF GOD

Now perhaps the first thing that may come to mind is the question; "So, what is grace and what does it mean to me as a Christian?" This is a very substantive question and a great starting place. Bible readers have probed the matter of grace in various ways. Some look at it in an academic way as a matter of theology that can be debated, while perhaps many only think of it as something mystical that nobody can understand, reducing it to a spiritual word that is somewhat irrelevant. Some simply identify grace as favor bestowed on those who have no merit. I submit that grace is a multifaceted outpoured measure of God's salvation that can be wonderfully realized and experienced in the life of a Christian.

Think with me about what Paul says in Ephesians 3:10. He speaks of the *"multifarious"* [many-sided or faceted] wisdom of God. I believe at the forefront of the multiple-sided wisdom is the aspect of the grace of God. While recently reading *"…where sin abounded, grace has super-abounded"* (Rom. 5:20 RV), I stopped to ponder what I had read. This phrase has caught the attention of countless Christians over the last two millennia, but that morning I was particularly drawn to meditate on the word super-abounded. A few weeks before this time, a couple had come to visit our home Bible-study. In the process of getting to know something about their experience of walking in fellowship with God, the brother mentioned that he had studied the matter of grace for ten years. I was considerably surprised by that. Studying some aspect of God's Word for that long, whether for doctrinal clarification or for spiritual enrichment, demonstrated a deep hunger that struck a chord in my own soul.

For a number of years, I had given a lot of thought to the matter of grace. The traditional definition of unmerited favor, though surely true, seemed to leave a sense of something not quite finished on the canvas of God's painting of my faith. I had studied the seven times that grace is referenced in 1 Peter and had been greatly blessed with Peter's presentation of grace *"being multiplied"* (1:2); the *"grace that is to be brought to you"* (1:10, 13); the *"grace of life"* (3:7); the *"manifold grace of God"* (4:10); *"the grace that He gives to the humble"* (5:5); the *"God of all grace"* (5:10); and the *"true grace of God in which we stand"* (5:12). Reading and rereading these verses created within me a whole new perspective of the functionality of grace in the Bible. There is so much richness in these verses. Yet, I had come short of experiencing the excellent provision that the biblical revelation presents to all believers by brother Peter. I began to realize that I want more and more of God's grace to operate in my life. But I had no understanding of the practicality and the functionality it was supposed to have in my normal Christian life.

Consider again the verse in Romans 5:20, *"grace has super-abounded."* What was Paul saying that I can practically lay hold of in my own life? How was this abounding grace to affect me in ways that I had not discovered? As I did this, a thought arose within my heart. *Herman, sin is temporal and limited, but grace is eternal and always expanding.* Grace is forever available and surpasses the momentary need. I believe that was a word from heaven. The more I meditated on these things, the more stirring there was in my spirit to investigate the part that grace plays in our salvation process. Somehow I suspected that the proper understanding of grace was going to make a significant change in my life as a believer.

A new desire for discovery had now arisen in my heart. Immediately, I began to pursue applications of the biblical presentation of grace. I longed to experience much more of what our God has provided as our inheritance of His salvation through Christ Jesus. I knew that I had not entered into a super-abounding grace relationship with God. I also knew that the help that I needed was in the words of the New Testament. So let us plunge into God's Word together and muse with the Holy Spirit over the first century believers' grace walk and our own experiences of grace. Let's see what we can discover in His presence!

In the beginning of the Gospel of John, he says this:

> *"...the Word became flesh and tabernacled among us (and we beheld His glory, glory as of the only Begotten of the Father), full of grace and truth... For, of His fullness we have all received, and grace upon grace. For the law was given through Moses; grace and reality came through Jesus Christ."*

(Jn. 1:14, 16)

This is really a powerful word. The law was something objective and outward. Grace came in the person of the Son of God. Think for a moment about John at the time of writing his gospel. John is an elderly man; he had probably read the other gospels; he had spent years walking in fellowship with the Lord. What he writes is very selective and purposeful. It is not like the other gospels in that it does not attempt to be chronological or historical. John reveals Jesus in a very particular way. He reveals Jesus as the divine Son of God, as the Word of life, as the Light of the world, and as the Lamb of God. The opening focus is that Jesus is God's Word, and as God speaking, He is full of grace. This is profoundly implying that the operation of God through Christ Jesus is in the element and flowing supply of grace. That flowing supply of grace is totally wrapped up in the person of Jesus. All the elements of the saving compassion and power of God are conveyed in Jesus.

It was in the predestined plan of God that through Jesus (the Son of God) God's full salvation would be transmitted to man through the factor of His grace. Consider how John describes Jesus here. He speaks of

One who is glorious in every imaginable way. Then he attaches the phrase, "full of grace." In addition, John says that of His fullness of grace and truth we have all received. This is almost incomprehensible to my natural mind. John is telling us that we have already received that much grace—fullness! Furthermore, this grace comes to us as "grace upon grace." My curiosity and excitement really gets stirred each time I read this. There is such a super abundant resource of grace in Jesus that it is described like endless rolling of waves upon a beach. By the life and redeeming death of Jesus Christ, we may receive grace to be justified and regenerated by God our Father! This grace comes to us as one wave follows another. I frequently rehearse these words in my meditation. I invite you to give John chapter 1 some of your quality time. Reading and rereading this chapter will allow the waves of grace to enlighten your understanding and enrich your fellowship with God.

There are seventy verses in the Old Testament where grace is mentioned and 103 in the New Testament. Since grace is mentioned so many times in the Bible, it is definitely a major theme in God's Word. For this writing, let's primarily focus on the verses in the New Testament which portray grace as God in transmission to His believers through Jesus Christ. There is a wide spectrum of grace throughout the New Testament. We will examine a number of verses that specifically mention grace and many others that define the practical outworking of grace as it is supplied to us and how it affects our relationship with God and everything. You may want to keep your Bible nearby in order to refer to these portions of Scripture.

Grace comes from our Father and the Lord Jesus Christ. It is to us all, and it is to be with our spirit. It is mentioned with peace in introductions. Three times Paul mentions grace and peace with mercy. Jude includes mercy with grace and peace as well. It is called the *"true grace of God,"* (1 Pet. 5:12) the *"grace of life,"* (1 Pet. 3:7) and described as *"great grace"* (Acts 4:33) which was upon all the saints in the church in Jerusalem. It is visible in as much as the effect of its operation is visible, *"...they had seen the grace"* (Acts 11:23). Grace is *"bestowed"* (2 Cor. 8:1) upon us; we are to be *"established"* (Heb. 13:9) in it; and we are *"heirs of the grace of life."* (1 Pet. 3:7)

As we pursue this subject in the Bible together, it is my hope to intensify your awareness of the love God demonstrates toward us. Keep in mind that this book is not intended to be an academic pursuit. I pray that your personal ability to lay hold of grace will grow and that your thanksgiving with praise to God our Father will increase superabundantly. God is full of grace. He wants to saturate us with His grace. That is what our Father's love is all about. As we receive this revelation, we will be Christians immersed in the grace of God and no longer under the demands of the law. We will see victory in Jesus because we will be being filled in our spirit, soul, and body with the fullness of His grace. We will be delivered from the frustrating entanglement of trying to serve God under the bondage of the law. Grace has so many facets that it perfectly fits every kind of need and situation. Whatever situations come into our lives, let us learn to face them with God's already supplied grace. Our God just cannot run out of grace! He has grace for every imaginable occasion.

CALLED BY HIS GRACE

Perhaps the appropriate starting point for us is to realize that we were called by God to enter into an amazing relationship with Him. God knew you before you were born and desired to bring you into His family and kingdom, so He started with a personal call to you. That calling is specific, purposeful, personal and saturated with grace.

> *"Then the word of the* LORD *came to me, saying: 'Before I formed you in the womb I knew you; before you were born I sanctified you;'"*
>
> (Jer. 1:4-5)

> *"And Jesus, walking by the Sea of Galilee, saw two brothers, Simon called Peter, and Andrew his brother, casting a net into the sea; for they were fishermen. Then He said to them, 'Follow Me and I will make you fishers of men.' They immediately left their nets and followed Him. Going on from there, He saw two other brothers, James the son of Zebedee, and John his brother, in the boat with Zebedee their father, mending their nets. He called them, and immediately they left the boat and their father, and followed Him."*
>
> (Matt. 4:18-22)

25

"But when it pleased God, who separated me from my mother's womb and called me through His grace, to reveal His Son in me, that I might preach Him among the Gentiles...."

(Gal. 1:15-16)

Perhaps you may think, "Well, these were special people; I am just a regular common person." Aren't fishermen regular folks? God called sheepherders (Moses and Amos). He called a money-loving schemer (Jacob), a prostitute (Rahab), and a tax collector (Matthew). Were not all of these regular people? Think about what Paul says in 1 Cor. 1:26-30.

"For you see your calling, brethren, that not many wise according to the flesh, not many mighty, not many noble, are called. But God has chosen the foolish things of the world to put to shame the wise, and God has chosen the weak things of the world to put to shame the things which are mighty; and the base things of the world and the things which are despised God has chosen, and the things which are not, to bring to nothing the things that are, that no flesh should glory in His presence."

God calls all kinds of men and women to be a part of His Kingdom. Do not allow the "deceiver" to trick you with thinking you're not worthy or something like the "I've been a really bad person" line. If you were worthy, you wouldn't need God's grace that brings you to salvation.

My own beginning was definitely a work of the grace of God. My father, Gabe Massey, and my mother,

Faye Jones, were both the youngest in large families. They were raised on farms in Texas. Each of them was born into a family that had for generations been strong Christians with a simple faith in God. But that didn't make me special to God. I was a person who needed to be saved by grace just like everyone else does. I was special to God simply because He wants me to be special to Him.

Dad and Mom met each other in their college years, and after five years of dating, they married. My older brother Taylor was born about a year and a half after that. Then a set of twins came along before Taylor was quite a year old. I was one of the twins; the other twin was brother Thurman. Thurman and Herman—for some reason people seem to find these names amusing.

God's grace was benevolently upon us from the very beginning. In Mom's late term pregnancy with us, she fell on some steps several weeks before her delivery date, and we twins had to be taken prematurely. Thurman and I weighed slightly over four pounds each. Our first several weeks were spent in an incubator in the hospital. In 1942 it was something of a miracle for babies to survive that kind of beginning. Taylor was a strong baby, but Thurman and I struggled through many illnesses for the first four to five years. I was the weaker of the two of us, though we both would frequently run a high fever and go into convulsions.

Listen to this story of God's grace. One late fall day in 1945, my dad was out of town on business, and a "blue norther" blew suddenly into Midland, Texas. We lived about five miles out of town and had some chickens and one cow that was about to drop her calf. Thurman and I were going through another illness, and I was having convulsions that night. The temperature outside began to drop below freezing very fast, which meant that the water in the water tank would soon freeze, leaving us without water until the storm passed.

Mother went outside to check on the cow and saw that the little shed where we kept the cow was on fire. Hay had begun to blow onto the roof of the house. Soon the roof of the house began to ignite. She told Taylor, who was five years old, to watch the twins while she went out to do whatever she could to put out the fires. We had no phone—it seemed that we were on our own. There was one water hose and a woman who knew how to cry out to God. Somehow by the visitation of the "great grace" of God, the fires were extinguished before the water froze in the water tank. The cow did not drop her calf, and neither Thurman nor I went into another convulsion. Indeed, that night the mercy and grace of God had overshadowed us.

A few years later, our family went on a fishing trip where we camped along the side of the river. This was always considered a magnificent way to spend time together in the summer. One morning while Dad was checking the trotlines and Mom was swimming, we three boys were playing in the river. I stepped off into a hole in the river and disappeared. No one noticed for a while until Mom saw my hair floating on the surface of the water. God, who was in control of everything, showed up. I was rescued from drowning that day. God had planned that I should grow up and learn to serve

Him in a number of ways, just like most of His children do. God wanted me to be a part of His family. He called me before I was born. His plan for my life was not to be cut short. By His grace He would bring me into that plan according to His calling. You are not any different. God wants you to fulfill His calling too. Therefore my friend, He has called you by His grace, and He will preserve you by His grace.

It doesn't matter who you are or what you may consider about yourself. If you have been born of God, you were called by His grace. God loves the whole world and wants all men to be saved. Will everyone respond positively to God's gracious call? The answer is no. But in John's gospel he said the following:

> *"He* [Jesus] *was in the world, and the world was made through Him, and the world did not know Him. He came to His own, and His own did not receive Him. But as many as received Him, to them He gave the right to become children of God, to those who believe in His name."*

(Jn. 1:10-12)

In sending His own son Jesus, God was calling everyone to come into an intimate relationship with Himself. This relationship is for all who will believe in Jesus. Perhaps a person may think, "Well that's not for me; I am useless and not smart, not a leader, and not especially gifted at anything," etc. All these things have nothing to do with God calling us. God has provided salvation for everyone to come to Him through Jesus. Grace is the means of that call. By grace we respond to that call. By grace we answer and live in the calling of God. For those who are called and respond by receiving Jesus as Savior, grace is a constant reality available to experience all the time, every day.

In 1964, while I was attending Baylor University, in Waco, Texas, I got to know an interesting young man. We will call him Buster Fillmycup. Buster had recently graduated from Wayland Baptist College in Plainview, Texas. Buster and I became very close friends and rented a small house together. As I got to know Buster, I found out that he had gotten "saved" in his childhood and later "surrendered" to God to become a preacher. In those formative stages of Christian growth, he was known to spread a map of the United States out before him and pray that God would use him in various states and places as he pointed to them on the map. Now Buster had grown up way out in west Texas. He looked like a west Texan and talked like a west Texan. Sometimes, I promise you, it seemed to me that he dressed almost like a hobo.

Buster had the worst West Texas accent you have ever heard or can imagine. I can remember him sitting in our living room and praying a number of times, "Lord, 'steer' (stir) us up!" He was skinny and tall. This man was what I imagined Ichabod Crane might have looked like. You might think that I held him in rather low esteem. That couldn't be further from the truth. In spite of all of his peculiarities, this brother was called of God. He said yes to Jesus, and grace was poured out upon him. Everyone that knew Buster loved him. This guy loved the Lord with all his heart. He was teachable although he had been a leader all of his life. Still, listening to him talk was an exercise in forbearance. Be all that as it may, God's grace called him. I say again, God in His grace called this man.

At the time of this writing, it has now been forty-seven years since I came to know Buster. There may be only two or three continents where Buster has not gone proclaiming the gospel of God and building up the churches there. As was said of the church in Jerusalem, "Great grace was upon them all." This is so true of my brother Buster, and it is absolutely, equally true of each one of us. God is no respecter of any persons! We all have received the abundance of His grace. Since we are called, we have a heritage of grace to receive, just like Buster. What shall we do? We must learn to let the grace of God do God's work in us and through us just like Buster has done.

Whether you experience the extensiveness of service like Buster or not is beside the point. I certainly have not! The point is this. God calls whom He wants to call. If you are born of God, you certainly got called by Him to be a significant part of what He is doing. Our God and Father, having called us by His grace, now wants us to grow and be established in the wonders of His grace. Step out in faith like Buster did! Lay hold of the grace of God who labors in your labor. Embrace with faith the words of Acts 14:3! *"Therefore they stayed there a long time, speaking boldly in the Lord, Who was bearing witness to the word of His grace, granting signs and wonders to be done by their hands."*

To the Thessalonian believers Paul admonished and encouraged them to be bold in the grace of their calling saying:

> *"For which also we pray always concerning you, that our God may count you worthy of your calling and may fulfill in power your every good intention for goodness and your work of faith, so that the name of our Lord Jesus may be glorified in you and you in Him, according to the grace of our God and the Lord Jesus Christ."*

(2 Thess. 1:11-12, RV)

The same expectation in prayer abides over each one of us who have been called of God. He is ready and able by His grace to fulfill in power your every good intention for goodness and your work of faith. Believe Him for this and rely on Him to do it through you according to your calling.

THE VASTNESS OF HIS GRACE

I have noticed that for a lot of Christians, grace seems to be somewhat abstract and illusive to the mind, perhaps just out of reach when it comes to practical things. In the light of the whole Scripture, grace is very real when seen in the arena of faith. Not only is it real, but it extends to limitlessness. It is not challenged by any problem, nor is it diminished by use. I say again: it is not diminished by use! Grace comes as our omnipotent, omniscient, omnipresent Father God activating salvation within us. As I studied and meditated over the verses in which grace appears, I discovered that grace is frequently used with strong verbs such as *"justified by grace, grace abounded and super-abounded, grace might reign, the grace labored, grace cause thanksgiving to abound, called by grace, saved by grace, glorified… according to the grace, grace…brings salvation…teaching us, grace is able to build you up, and give you an inheritance, and grow in grace."* It also appears in phrases like *"My grace is sufficient, be established by grace, grace be multiplied, be strong in the grace, grace given to you, receive grace, grace that would come to you, and grace that is brought to you."* It is linked with profound nouns like *"the word of His grace, the election of grace, the dispensation of grace, exceeding riches of, the gift of, the throne of, and the Spirit of grace."* Our personal participation with grace is revealed as *"your words…impart grace," "let your speech be with grace," "sing with grace in your heart," "and partakers with me of grace."* It appears in phrases as *"grace of life," "true grace," "and all grace."* The range that grace traverses encompasses the need of every person on earth and throughout all time.

This brief overview shows us how God's administration is permeated with grace. His fullness is supplied and manifested to us through His grace. Consider it prayerfully. Reviewing the adjoining words and phrases is very helpful. Let your mind adsorb how far-reaching grace expands to enrich our lives with Christ in daily practical matters. God's intention and good pleasure is to rescue mankind and restore all men to His original plan. The Bible reveals the central role grace occupies in the salvation process and how thoroughly the process is wrapped in the operation of grace.

Let me insert one caution here. We readers of the Bible are sometimes so familiar with the biblical language that when we read the Bible, we may fail to experience the impact of its emancipating reality. We must learn to let these words settle down into our hearts as they are written and allow the divine Word to do His operation of revealing. I will focus on this in more detail in chapters 3 and 5.

Grace is always accessible and available through the *"word of His grace."* When we read the Bible, the Holy Spirit is breathing over us to impart enlightenment, revelation, emancipation, assurance, victory, and supply. Whenever we connect with the *"Spirit of grace"* with our human spirit, our mind will be renewed and filled with divine understanding. This is what I mean when speaking of the vastness of grace. Grace knows no limitation. It is inexhaustible and is not reduced by use. When it is tested, it is always found absolutely reliable. It surpasses every challenge with ease because it releases the divine attributes of the Creator. By employing grace, we are progressively being *"saved by grace,"* as the saving life of Jesus flows to us and through us. In moments of our human need, we are being delivered from the *"old man"* and transported into a living in the realm of the *"new man,"* the new creation of God in Christ.

Grace is so vast and so innately saturated with God's nature and character that when it comes to us and we apply it, faith arises—our perceptions change in the light of what Christ has already done for us. God's ability is administered in our human circumstances.

> *"And my God shall supply all your need according to His riches in glory by Christ Jesus. Now to our God and Father be glory forever and ever. Amen."*

(Phil. 4:19-20)

Did you notice that the verse says that God is supplying us not according to all our need? He is supplying us according to His riches in Christ Jesus! That's vast! That's really over the top! I hope that you are connecting with this. I'm reveling in it!

NOBODY SPECIAL

In 1974, my wife, Kathleen, and I were living in Austin, Texas. Many of the members in our local church were active in sharing the gospel to young people who hung out on the "Drag" by the University of Texas. A significant number of young men and women had believed in Christ through this evangelistic labor. Among them were some people who were living on the street or in unhealthy or immoral situations. Kathleen and I opened our home to several of these newly saved kids in order to take care of them and nurture their progress in the faith.

During that time in Austin, a wonderful young man came to live with us. We will call him Mic Brolove. Mic had joined the navy shortly after graduating from high school. He was a diligent and bright young man, but Mic was so introverted that he was extremely inse-cure in large groups. That would be a group of three or more. His communication skills were held in bondage by his insecurities. Mic was born again when he came to us and had been under some Christian training by the Navigators, which is an organization much like Campus Crusade.

Mic appeared unusually nervous when the spotlight was on him to speak or pray extemporaneously in pub-lic. In our church meetings there was always extended time reserved for people to give testimonies about their experiences of Christ in their daily lives. If Mic ven-tured to give a testimony, that was indeed a risk beyond the pale for him. After such an attempt, which was really rare, poor Mic would go into a fog of introspec-tion. "Did I say it right?" "Did I spend too much time trying to make my point?" "Did I leave something out that I should have said?" If you don't know this dun-geon of spiritual danger, just try to imagine it.

Over time, we discovered that Mic had a blessed ability to memorize portions of scripture and hymns. Sometimes, in our home meetings, he would just burst out with a bunch of verses that were amazingly appro-priate and helpful to us all. The same thing would happen with hymns. Even now, as I recall this amaz-ing growth in Mic, in my spirit I hear Paul's words in Romans 11:33: *"Oh, the depth of the riches both of the wisdom and knowledge of God! How unsearchable are His judgments and His ways past finding out!"* Another ordi-nary person had laid hold on the grace that was able to build him up in Christ Jesus.

He would quote a hymn or suggest we sing it. Whatever he did, it seemed to be what we all needed at the time. I remember at first when this would happen, some of us would sneak a peek at each other with that sideways glance, "Is this Mic?" *Yep!* Mic was learning a lot at Jesus' side, and Jesus was transmitting grace to us through this renewed earthen vessel. Soon he was playing his guitar and leading our singing. 1 Peter 2:9-10 describes our brother so well:

> *"But you are a chosen generation, a royal priesthood, a holy nation, His own special people, that you may proclaim the praises of Him who called you out of darkness into His marvelous light; who once were not a people but are now the people of God, who had not obtained mercy but now have obtained mercy."*

By the way, God's grace poured out on Mic in another way. He gave Mic a beautiful, God-loving wife and two daughters. These daughters are grown now but have already spread a lot of Jesus' love, joy, and peace to a lot of folks. In my opinion, these girls are really marvelously blessed. God's grace is surely upon them. What God's grace had begun in Mic passed on to the next generation.

I should mention that Mic for many years has been a very gifted electrician and a well recognized teacher and trainer of people who are entering that craft. He loves teaching and has no inhibitions in making his presentations. And I am told that his classes are outstanding. He also has his own business building circuit boards for computer operated equipment.

Today, Mic still astonishes me. He is continually bringing a rich portion of his daily Christian experiences into our fellowship. It is apparent to everyone that Christ is his life. He has learned to:

> *"Let the word of Christ dwell in you richly in all wisdom, teaching and admonishing one another in psalms and hymns and spiritual songs, singing with grace in your hearts to the Lord. And whatever you do in word or deed, do all in the name of the Lord Jesus, giving thanks to God the Father through Him."*

(Col. 3:16-17)

This is a common example of what grace can do in ordinary folks. By the way, Mic has said "goodbye" to that demonic debilitating self consciousness. He is truly made free in Jesus. What he could not do for himself, God did for him by grace abounding. Hallelujah!

THE SAME GRACE FOR US ALL

In Romans, chapters 3, 4, and 5, when Paul is describing the operation of grace, he defines an irrevocable principal. We cannot rely on anything that we do to establish a relationship with God except believe in and receive Jesus by simple faith. This amazing grace is the same for all believers and is available to all who believe in Jesus. Let's consider Paul's presentation in the following verses:

"...being justified freely by His grace through the redemption that is in Christ Jesus, (3:24);

For if Abraham was justified by works, he has something to boast about, but not before God. For what does the Scripture say? 'Abraham believed God and it was accounted to him for righteousness. Now to him who works, the wages are not counted as grace but as debt.' (4:2-4);

Therefore it is of faith that it might be according to grace, so that the promise might be sure to all the seed, not only to those who are of the law, but also to those who are of the faith of Abraham, who is the father of us all. (4:16-17);

Therefore, having been justified by faith, we have peace with God through our Lord Jesus Christ, through whom also we have access by faith into this grace in which we stand, and rejoice in hope of the glory of God (5:1-2);

But the free gift is not like the offense. For if by the one man's offense many died, much more the grace of God and the gift by the grace of the one Man, Jesus Christ, abounded to many....For if by the one man's offense death reigned through the one, much more those who receive abundance of grace and of the gift of righteousness will reign in life through the One, Jesus Christ. (5:15,17);

Moreover the law entered that the offense might abound. But where sin abounded, grace abounded much more [Greek—super-abounded], *so that as sin reigned in death, even so grace might reign through righteousness to eternal life through Jesus Christ our Lord."* (5:20-21)

In these verses Paul is laying the sure foundation regarding God's saving work by faith based on grace. Human effort to fulfill the law is a vain religious attempt to become righteous before God. Jesus Christ Himself is the unique manifestation of God's grace. We come to God only through Him. Jesus said, *"I am the way, the truth and the life. No one comes to the Father but by me."* (John 14:6) Grace is the sphere of what God has done in Christ to provide salvation for man. We are now in that blessed sphere! Faith in His work is the unique and exclusive way to come to God. If you have not taken that step of faith in what God has done for you, I sincerely invite you to do it now. Simply tell God that you thank Him for sending Jesus to bear the judgment for your sins for you when He died on the cross. Tell Him that you now know that you need to be saved from the condemnation that comes from the sins you have committed. Tell Him that you believe that Jesus has done this for you and that you receive Him as your Savior.

Paul wrote, *"The grace of God that brings us salvation has appeared to all men."* (Titus 2:11) The Greek word for *"salvation,"* is in the "sozo" word family. The verb "sozo" means to save, to preserve, keep from harm, to heal, and to deliver. Now that is a mighty inclusive word full of benefits. It is by God's grace that such divine intervention occurs in human circumstances. In the creation of man, God had a profound mission for the man He formed with His own hands. This man was then animated by God's own breath. Sound familiar? On the evening of Christ's resurrection, Jesus breathed on His disciples and said to them, *"Receive the Holy Spirit."* (John 20:22) The mission that God had originally planned for man was to replenish the earth with God-related and God-focused men and women. Adam, Eve, and their children were to *"keep"* the garden of God and to subdue the Satan-dominated earth. Satan realized that this God-centered man would be his demise. Therefore he enticed Adam and Eve to disobey God, thus postponing the divine mission. Consequently, the depravity of man began to set in as Satan's deceptive nature corrupted man's thoughts and behavior. God, however, did not abandon His purpose for man.

After four thousand years of human failure to attain to the righteousness of God, a new man entered the scene. This man was Jesus, the son of God and son of man. The divine and the human nature were perfectly joined together. Jesus as a man was the *"last Adam"* and the *"second man."* (1 Cor. 15:45, 47) He was born of a virgin and raised in the humble home of a carpenter. The story is told in Matthew, chapter 1, and Luke, chapter 2. That Christmas story is known and celebrated throughout the world. In Hebrews and Philippians, however, there are some marvelous details of the incarnation that are not so well known.

Hebrews 10:5-7, 10 says,

> *"Therefore, when He came into the world, He said: 'Sacrifice and offering You did not desire, but a body You have prepared for Me. In burnt offerings and sacrifices for sin You had no pleasure. Then I said, 'Behold, I have come —In the volume of the book it is written of Me —To do Your will, O God.'…By that will we have been sanctified through the offering of the body of Jesus Christ once for all."*

In Philippians 2:5-11 Paul says,

> *"…Christ Jesus, who, being in the form of God, did not consider it robbery to be equal with God, but made Himself of no reputation, taking the form of a bondservant, and coming in the likeness of men. And being found in appearance as a man, He humbled Himself and became obedient to the point of death, even the death of the cross. Therefore God also has highly exalted Him and given Him the name which is above every name, that at the name of Jesus every knee should bow, of those in heaven, and of those on earth, and of those under the earth, and that every tongue should confess that Jesus Christ is Lord, to the glory of God the Father."*

The more I mused over these verses, a revelation broke upon my consciousness of the deep desire and love for mankind that is awesomely demonstrated in the incarnation of Jesus. God passionately desires to reestablish an intrinsic relationship with all men. Jesus Christ became the ultimate all-inclusive demonstration of the love of God poured out to regain mankind.

God's love is revealed through verses like the following:

> *"God so loved the world that He gave His only begotten Son that whoever believes in Him should not perish but should have eternal life."*

(John 3:16)

God has reached out to recover man to His original purpose for him. This is reiterated in Paul's letter to Titus. *"The grace of God that brings us salvation has appeared to all men."* (Titus 2:11) Paul spoke of his personal experience of this grace that reached him in Galatians 1:15, telling us: *"But when it pleased God, who separated me from my mother's womb and called me through His grace to reveal His Son in me, that I might preach Him among the Gentiles…."* The love of God compelled Him to intervene in the events of time to rescue and reclaim man from his estranged condition. He sent Jesus into the world, full of grace, to save us.

Paul is a good example of salvation's work. He was formerly a religious zealot who persecuted Christians and was responsible for having many murdered, but God called Paul to a predestinated mission. God described it to Ananias in Acts 9:15, *"But the Lord said to him [Ananias], 'Go, for he is a chosen vessel of Mine to bear My name before Gentiles, kings, and the children of Israel.'"* Every believer in Jesus has a calling upon him to come and enter into this salvation and to participate in a special divine partnership with God. That partnership is to establish the kingdom of God on earth. Only you can fulfill your unique calling of God. To interact with God in this partnership is one of the central themes included in being *"saved."* The divine calling is uniquely yours to discover, explore, and fulfill. The range, the scope of what this inherently includes is as mind boggling as the pictures captured by the Hubble telescope. All this is grace in action. It is all entirely in Jesus Christ. It is for you, for me, and for everyone who will believe in Jesus.

Think about the time when you heard the call of God in your life. Did you become aware of the dimensions of grace that awaited you? That sensation is the grace of God poured out into you. Peter spoke of the *"multiplied grace"* of God (1 Pet 1:2) that is coming to you. Have you considered how much God has prepared and planned to do for you and through you? He wants to open your understanding to the highest level of His aspiration for you individually. By the victory of Jesus, our heavenly Father broke through the darkness that had held your mind captive to the devil and the world. From birth everyone is held captive by the devil in bondage to sin and darkness. 2 Corinthians 4:3-4 tells us, *"But even if our gospel is veiled, it is veiled to those who are perishing, whose minds the god of this age has blinded, who do not believe, lest the light of the gospel of the glory of Christ, who is the image of God, should shine on them."*

It is written in Acts 10:38 Jesus came to release all those who were being oppressed by the devil. God selected you long before you had any sense of your need for salvation. Then by the shining of His light into your heart,

"…you heard Him and were taught by Him as the truth is in Jesus."

(Eph 4:21)

The Bible says that God *"…called us with a holy calling, not according to our works, but according to His own purpose and grace which was given to us in Christ Jesus…."* (2 Tim 1:9) Grace transmitted the call into our heart through the Holy Spirit, bringing us the faith to believe and respond to His call. All this is grace in operation, applying the love of God through faith. Now you can respond by saying, "Yes Lord, I believe and receive all that You are as Savior and all You have done to save me!" That salvation, according to His calling, includes many items. Romans chapter 6 sums it up quite well. I urge you to read it often. Read it slowly, and let the Holy Spirit inscribe on your heart the rich truth that is there. Absorb the intrinsic value that has been secured for you through His saving grace.

SAVED BY GRACE

Ephesians chapter 2 is a magnificent window that enables us to see into God's heart of love in relation to our experience of the saving grace of God. To believe in Jesus is to escape the judgment of God and the resulting wrathful condemnation that sends a soul to everlasting separation from God. *"Saved by grace"*—even the sound of the words is heavenly and resounds with a sense of hope and security. It is not surprising that the hymn "Amazing Grace" is so stirring to hearts around the world. It moves, inspires, and comforts both singer and listener. How much do we Christians embrace the *"riches of His grace"* in our daily experience of salvation? Don't you think that there is a lot more of salvation awaiting your discovery? It is by faith that man accesses and appropriates all that grace affords. Let's get started by looking at Ephesians chapter 2 and allow the Holy Spirit to teach us how amazing God's grace is.

> *"And you He made alive, who were dead in trespasses and sins, in which you once walked according to the course of this world, according to the prince of the power of the air, the spirit who now works in the sons of disobedience, among whom also we all once conducted ourselves in the lusts of our flesh, fulfilling the desires of the flesh and of the mind, and were by nature children of wrath, just as the others. But God who is rich in mercy, because of His great love with which He loved us, even when we were dead in trespasses, made us alive together with Christ (by grace you have been saved), and raised us up together, and made us sit together in the heavenly places in Christ Jesus, that in the ages to come He might show the exceeding riches of His grace in His kindness toward us in Christ Jesus. For by grace you have been saved through faith, and that not of yourselves; it is the gift of God, not of works, lest anyone should boast. For we are His workmanship, created in Christ Jesus for good works, which God prepared beforehand that we should walk in them. Therefore remember that you, once Gentiles in the flesh—who are called Uncircumcision by what is called the Circumcision*

> *made in the flesh by hands—that at that time you*
> *were without Christ, being aliens from the com-*
> *monwealth of Israel and strangers from the cove-*
> *nants of promise, having no hope and without God*
> *in the world. But now in Christ Jesus you who once*
> *were far off have been brought near by the blood of*
> *Christ."*

(Eph. 2:1-13)

Who can read this and think that we can do anything to save ourselves? How can anyone read of such
compassion with wisdom and purpose and not be
stirred with a sensation of awe? We were totally alien-
ated from God and without hope. God saw us in our
hopelessness yet loved us anyway. Our sinfulness, even
our deadness, could not inhibit God from saving us
through His work manifested in Jesus at the cross.
Only our refusal to believe in Jesus can stop this from
becoming ours. No human endeavor can elevate us into
the purpose and presence of God. Paul told his co-
worker Timothy about this in 2 Timothy 1:8-10.

> *"…God, who has saved us and called us with a holy*
> *calling, not according to our works, but according*
> *to His own purpose and grace which was given to*
> *us in Christ Jesus before time began, but has now*
> *been revealed by the appearing of our Savior Jesus*
> *Christ, who has abolished death and brought life*
> *and immortality to light through the gospel."*

There is not one thing that we could do to help ourselves, much less save ourselves as far as God is concerned. It is His purpose to save us; it is by His grace

that He does it! We need God to undertake for us; apart from His work in Jesus, we are without hope. Our hope is conceived in the love of God which was transmitted to us through His grace. That grace came to us in Jesus. On earth, from the beginning of our pilgrimage with God to the end of it, we shall be the objects and the work of His grace. This grace is God in action to produce faith and praise in us. Thus we truly are God's *"masterpiece"* (Eph. 2:10).

In the Old Testament book of Zechariah the finality of the work of God through grace was foretold by saying,

> *"This is the word of the* LORD *to Zerubbabel: 'Not by might nor by power, but by My Spirit' Says the* LORD *of hosts 'Who are you, O great mountain* [God's enemies]? *Before Zerubbabel you shall become a plain! And he shall bring forth the capstone* [Jesus Christ] *with shouts of 'Grace, grace to it!'"*

(Zech. 4:6-7)

I contemplate what is said at the end of these verses, and I am reassured that it is by grace that we participate in the purpose of God. My brother-in-law once said, "When I get to heaven, I will not be saying, 'Wow! I made it'. Rather I will say, 'I'm here only by the grace of God.'" I don't think that it can be more perfectly stated.

In the Old Testament, God required the blood of a lamb to cover the sins of man. Through this sacrifice of blood, the sins of the people were covered in order to provide a way for man to approach God without invoking His judgment and wrath. This wrathful judgment occurs because the holiness and righteousness of God are offended by sin. Apart from this blood atonement, God could not draw near to man, and neither could man draw near to God. The lamb was only a temporary prototype of the coming Messiah—Jesus Christ. Concerning the coming of the son of God/son of man, Hebrews 1 and John 1 reveal to us further details of the Lamb of God from the divine side.

Hebrews 1:1-3 declares,

> *"God, who at various times and in various ways spoke in time past to the fathers by the prophets, has in these last days spoken to us by His Son, whom He has appointed heir of all things, through whom also He made the worlds; who being the brightness of His glory and the express image of His person, and upholding all things by the word of His power, when He had by Himself purged our sins, sat down at the right hand of the Majesty on high."*

John 1:14 says, *"And the Word became flesh and dwelt among us, and we beheld His glory, the glory as of the only begotten of the Father."*

Jesus as the Lamb of God accomplished all that was required in God's ultimate plan of salvation. John proclaimed, *"Behold! The Lamb of God who takes away the sin of the world."* (Jn. 1:29) After His perfect human living, the crucifixion, resurrection, and ascension of Jesus the Christ, all was finished. Redemption was secured for man. Comparing this with chapter 2 of Paul's letter to the Ephesians brings me into a better understanding of the process of God saving us through His grace. I worship God, contemplating the depth of His love and wisdom that is manifested in Jesus.

The preceding verses review salvation from man's side. These verses will enrich your faith through repeated reading with prayerful meditation. It is not sufficient to reach a mental understanding here. Salvation is a personal matter resulting in a very subjective living and growing relationship between God and each of us. Each of us must personalize and internalize the promises of God in the Bible. You and I will benefit greatly by meditating on *"the word of His grace, which is able to build you up and give you an inheritance among all those who are sanctified"* (Acts 20:32) until it is immovable from our consciousness. No knowledge about God can substitute for this personal knowledge of God. Through such confident awareness, each party participates in the love and interaction of the other. A transcendent mutuality in communion awaits our vigorous pursuit!

I am compelled to address a doctrinal issue here. Some denominations insist that one may fall from grace. What they mean by this is that one who is saved may become "unsaved." I believe this is an exceedingly deceptive error. First of all, if one is born of God, how can he become "unborn" of God? After viewing all the wonders of God's work of grace, how can one speculate that God as our Father can or would change His nature and character to become unreliable regarding our salvation? Since He accomplished everything in the life and work of Christ, can He somehow turn His back on all that and condemn one of His children? Certainly not! The parable of the *"prodigal son"* in Luke 15:11-32 declares the heart of the Father is instinctively to forgive and to restore. That is unchangeable!

To "fall from grace" is not to be cast into perdition. It is to turn from what God has done for us in Jesus and to try to use some other means to relate to God. It is to receive the grace of God but not use it. That is the height of foolishness. To do so is to abandon grace and not use it; it is to go back to the law of Moses or some human pursuit to have a relationship with God. Why would anyone do that? Many have and many do. Let's look at Paul's language to the believers in the Galatian churches.

Paul is saying, "Look Galatians saints, you were running well and gaining supernal heights through the grace God was supplying." What happened? Read his words in Galatians 3:1-3:

> *"O foolish Galatians! Who has bewitched you that you should not obey the truth, before whose eyes Jesus Christ was clearly portrayed among you as crucified? This only I want to learn from you: Did you receive the Spirit by the works of the law, or by the hearing of faith? Are you so foolish? Having begun in the Spirit, are you now being made perfect by the flesh?"*
>
> *"I marvel that you are turning away so soon from Him who called you in the grace of Christ, to a different gospel, which is not another; but there are some who trouble you and want to pervert the gospel of Christ. But even if we, or an angel from*

heaven, preach any other gospel to you than what we have preached to you, let him be accursed."

(Gal. 1:6-8)

"For I through the law died to the law that I might live to God. I have been crucified with Christ; it is no longer I who live, but Christ lives in me; and the life which I now live in the flesh I live by faith in [Greek—"of"] *the Son of God, who loved me and gave Himself for me. I do not set aside the grace of God; for if righteousness comes through the law, then Christ died in vain."*

(Gal. 2:19-21)

Law keeping is revealed as self effort to establish righteousness on our own. In Galatians 5:1, Paul says, *"Stand fast therefore in the liberty by which Christ has made us free, and do not be entangled again with a yoke of bondage* [anything other than Christ Jesus].*"* That yoke is to try to fulfill the requirements of the law rather than to appropriate the work of God in Christ.

"Indeed I, Paul, say to you that if you become circumcised, Christ will profit you nothing. And I testify again to every man who becomes circumcised that he is a debtor to keep the whole law. You have become estranged from Christ, you who attempt to be justified by law; you have fallen from grace. For, we through the Spirit eagerly wait for the hope of righteousness by faith. For in Christ Jesus neither

circumcision nor uncircumcision avails anything, but faith working through love."

(Gal. 5:2-6)

On the other hand, those who proclaim that one who is once saved is always saved may fail to see the depth, length, height, and breadth of what it means to "be saved." These folks probably are speaking of going to heaven. Indeed that is a viable part of salvation's provision, but it is not the whole. This thinking and preaching is far too shallow. Going to heaven is not the unique goal for Christians. God wants us to live by Christ's life here on earth now and be conformed into His image, here and now. Going to heaven is something like the frosting on the cake.

When we look into the matter of God's plan of salvation and what is included, we will be overwhelmed with the extent to which salvation has to do with our living in the here and now on this earth. God wants men and women living in victory over sin, flesh, self, the world, demonic activity, and Satan on this earth now—thus demonstrating the kingdom of God. If, after being born again, a Christian lives like the ungodly, unregenerate person, there will be dire consequences at the judgment seat of Christ. Romans 14:10 says, *"But why do you judge your brother? Or why do you show contempt for your brother? For we shall all stand before the judgment seat of Christ."* And 2 Corinthians 5:9-11 says,

> *"Therefore, we make it our aim, whether present or absent, to be well pleasing to Him. For we must all appear before the judgment seat of Christ, that*

*each one may receive the things done in the body,
according to what he has done, whether good or
bad. Knowing, therefore, the terror of the Lord, we
persuade men; but we are well known to God, and
I also trust are well known in your consciences."*

These verses declare plainly that there will be a judgment wherein Christians are examined by Christ. This examination is to establish the matter of reward for living in the grace of God given to each one. It has nothing to do with losing our salvation or being cast into eternal perdition. I urge the saints of God who have lived under the security of the believer doctrine not to be careless in your living this life. Do not think that all is fine because you have your "ticket to heaven." There is much more to the Christian life than just escaping hell. This kind of thinking and living is dangerously near to, if not in reality, *"setting aside the grace of God"* (Gal. 2:21). God's grace has so much to do with our life and living now. His will is that we would live in victory now. That is what is well pleasing to Him. Remember it is His good pleasure to save us.

Saved—it is so meaningful! How much do we children of God grasp what is included and provided in salvation? Exploring this will thrill the heart! Salvation has its objective and subjective side. The objective side consists of all that God has done for us to secure salvation for man. The subjective side is our experiential entering into what God has accomplished for us. Remember that everything God has done on the objective side of salvation is in the sphere of grace as unmerited favor, and we may now appropriate this grace with all its value and benefits by faith (Rom. 4:16). That is the subjective side of grace for the believer. The more we access by faith God's grace with all its saving potential, the more we draw near to God, and God draws near to us.

Do you see the mutuality here? God wants to save us—we need to be saved by Him. He has done everything that salvation requires. We only need to believe and receive by faith what awaits us. To receive is to invite Jesus to come into our life. How foolish is it to think that one can improve on what God has done? To be saved by grace is simply to agree with what God accomplished in Christ. We cannot do something to earn it. It is His gift. I remember so clearly what the Lord spoke into my heart one day. "Herman, never be confused about this matter of grace. Grace is my giving, not My payment, as if I owe you something."

LEARNING TO PRACTICE

A few years ago, I had begun to arise in the middle of the night to pray. During these times I purposed to do nothing but to commune in prayer with God. I had not yet come to know God as Father very well at all, but I was soon to discover Him. During these times of prayer, I would sometimes kneel, sometimes prostrate myself, but always the time was spent with me doing all the talking. I told Him about my concerns, my friends, my family, my financial needs, the needs of the members in our local church, etc. These vigils usually lasted for more than an hour. One night, I was pouring out my requests and concerns when I was interrupted. "If this is supposed to be a conversation, why don't you let Me say something?" I didn't move! It wasn't an audible voice that I heard with my physical ears, but I had heard His voice in my soul. Suddenly, I had nothing to say.

That voice was so calming and at the same time, it was so persuasive, authoritative, yet affectionate. I was captivated, longing to hear more. I was afraid to do anything lest I disturb the atmosphere and lose this special moment. For what seemed a half hour, but was probably ten minutes, I remained motionless, trying to clear my mind of everything. I didn't want to miss anything, even if it were a single word. No more words came. There was only stillness and quietness. Even so, I don't think I had ever experienced such tranquility as I did at that moment. Then my Heavenly Father began to speak to me again. I don't remember any details of that conversation, but I remember my sensation. It was like when two people begin to get to know each other. I didn't need to inform or coach Him anymore because He knew me so well already. It was He that was unknown to me.

For however long the encounter lasted, I was captivated. Then I knew that it was over. The next night, I eagerly awaited another visitation. I got up as usual and sat on the floor at the end of my bed. I waited and waited, struggling to reject any and all thoughts that tried to occupy my mind. Nothing happened. For what may have been between fifteen and twenty minutes, I waited and began to grow sleepy. I resisted the sleep, feeling confident that my Father would speak to me again. I was trying so hard to reconstruct what had happened the night before. At last, in my heart, it seemed that He was assuring me with the message, "I am here." Lingering for a few more minutes, I realized that it was time to go back to bed. Counterfeiting doesn't work with God, no matter how sincere one may be. These vigils continued for weeks. The conversations grew longer, and were so very personal in details. I was getting acquainted with the God of *"all grace who called us to His eternal glory by Christ Jesus…."* (1 Pet. 5:10)

One imperative detail that I quickly learned was to quiet my soul. By this I mean that I had to clear my mind and heart of everything. This was not yoga or anything like transcendental meditation. No, it was the realization that I could easily imagine something like the divine words with something concocted out of my own corrupt mind. I am confident that you have had the experience of trying to pray and your mind gets flooded with all kinds of stuff. That is frustrating and annoying. After some extended nights of fellowship, I learned that it was far more profitable to let the Father do most of the speaking. What a turn of events! So much of my praying seemed to be chattering at Him rather than learning from Him. There are many verses in John's gospel that portray the intimacy that Jesus had with God the Father. God wants to experience the same intimacy with you and me. Simply draw near to Him, and you will find that fellowship with God no longer seems unreal or beyond your personal participation. God is so available to you. It is as if you were the only child He has to talk to and to care for.

James 4:8 says, *"Draw near to God and He will draw near to you. Cleanse your hands, you sinners; and purify your hearts, you double-minded."* James goes on to say in verse 10, *"Humble yourselves in the sight of the Lord, and He will lift you up."* Be careful here. Don't get caught up in working to qualify yourself to be with God. He wants this communion far more than you can imagine. I believe that to cleanse your hands and purify your heart here is to remove everything else from your mind. It is almost impossible to hear Him when the roar of this world's demands is coursing through your brain. These words of James helped me a great deal because they defined for me what I had been experiencing. Another reason I spoke very little was because I wanted to really get to know Abba, a Hebrew title of endearment for father much like our word daddy. I learned that I could not constrain Him to speak; neither did I want to initiate a topic. I am the learner; Abba is my teacher through His Holy Spirit. Mostly, I waited for Him. Whenever He began to communicate, the throne of grace was before me. Jesus, full of grace and truth, had brought me to Abba.

Do you remember Paul's words in Philippians 3:7-10? He said,

> *"But what things were gain to me, these I have counted loss for Christ. Yet indeed I also count all things loss for the excellence of the knowledge of Christ Jesus my Lord, for whom I have suffered the loss of all things, and count them as rubbish, that I*

may gain Christ and be found in Him, not having
my own righteousness, which is from the law, but
that which is through faith in Christ, the right-
eousness which is from God by faith; that I may
know Him and the power of His resurrection, and
the fellowship of His sufferings...."

I wasn't there yet. Neither am I there now, but this is one thing of which I am sure. I am closer than ever before. I am reflecting the cry of Paul's heart. I am entering into the kingdom of God—the rule of God where grace reigns.

To me this is the substance of the gospel. It is not merely a story. It is the really good news of heaven and earth. At the same time, it was not something that I found easy to talk about. Was this too mystical and strange for others to hear? Perhaps! I was learning like a child, and to try to tell someone else was just impossible. Words were inadequate; my mind seemed to fail me to find reasonable language. I hesitantly made occasional modest attempts to share my venture of grace with my wife. She would listen with sincere interest, but I have no idea what may have made sense to her. This was simply the grace of God given to me, for me. And you know what? There is plenty for you too! I had begun to "...*set my hope fully upon the grace that is to be brought...*" to me (1 Pet. 1:13). Over time, my soul could confirm John's words in his first epistle. He says,

"That which we have seen and heard we declare
to you, that you also may have fellowship with us;
and truly our fellowship is with the Father and

with His Son Jesus Christ. And these things we write to you that your joy may be full."

(1 Jn. 1:3-4)

I am one among myriads who are learning what Paul spoke of as *"the grace of God bestowed on the churches"* (2 Cor. 8:1).

CHAPTER 2

THE OPERATION OF GRACE

Grace 'tis a charming sound,
Harmonious to the ear;
Heav'n with the echo shall resound,
And all the earth shall hear.

'Twas grace that wrote my name
In life's eternal book:
'Twas grace that gave me to the Lamb,
Who all my sorrows took.

Grace taught my wandering feet
To tread the pilgrim road;
And new supplies each hour I meet
While pressing on to God.

Grace taught my heart to pray,
And made my eyes o'erflow;
'Tis grace which kept me to this day,
And will not let me go.

Grace all the work shall crown
Through everlasting days;
It lays in love the topmost stone
And well deserves the praise.

Oh, let that grace inspire
My heart with strength divine;
May all my powers to Thee aspire,
And all my days be Thine.

(Augustus M. Toplady, *Hymns,*
Living Stream Ministry, Anaheim, CA, 1966)

This song has greatly enriched the lives of many saints. It has facilitated their ability to rely on the grace of God to carry them into a deeper walk in His presence. It relays the message of assurance and confident hope that God wants to get deeply integrated into our whole life existence. God labored through His grace to do everything that was needed to secure our complete redemption. Now by the same grace of God, all that He has done is accessible to us. I've said this before, but it is worth repeating.

In order to understand the operation of grace and how we are impacted by it, we need to look at the verses where grace is connected with action verbs.

For example, we were justified freely by His grace. To resolve the sin impasse, God sent His Son Jesus to take away our sins.

> *"Behold the Lamb of God who takes away the sin of the world."*

(Jn. 1:29)

Because God is holy and righteous in His nature, it would be unjust for Him to allow unholy, unrighteous people to enter into His presence. This sinful condition became the obstacle to overcome for both God and man. Man certainly couldn't bridge the gap, so God did it. Because Jesus lived perfectly before God as a man, He could bring His holy and righteous humanity to God on behalf of all mankind. Jesus was the real Lamb of God Who could perfectly satisfy all the just requirements of God's divine nature.

We who have believed into Christ Jesus have been justified by the grace of God because this abounding grace has the human living of Jesus in it. This is extremely important to us in our practical human living. We are in the process of being saved in the fullest meaning of the Greek word "sozo." Along our journey, we sin and fall short of living in the victory of the life of Jesus. At once the *"accuser"* (Satan) descends upon us to accuse us of failure and condemns our faith as unreal, thus confusing our mind. All of us can relate to this as Christians. God has justified us! That is not temporary or conditional. The work of salvation cannot be rescinded or overthrown. We are still justified before God by the saving life of Christ in spite of our failures and disobedient actions. On our side, we are still committing sin. On God's side, He always extends grace to forgive our sin. At this time our conscience may be cleared and freed by confessing our sin and acknowledging the truth of God's grace.

"If we confess our sins, He is faithful and just to forgive us our sins and to cleanse us from all unrighteousness."

(1 Jn. 1:9)

Regardless of what we feel or how fierce the devil's assault, God says we are justified. Whom shall we believe? How shall we personally apply this and experience the freedom that comes from knowing the truth that sets us free? The answer resolutely is to believe and receive the truth that is in Jesus. Never be confused by the enemy Satan. He comes to steal, kill and destroy. (Jn. 10:10) Rev. 12:10 tells us that Satan accuses us day and night, but we overcome him by the blood of the Lamb and the word of our testimony. This word of our testimony is more than just proclaiming *"the truth that is in Jesus."* It also is our faith as we live in the power of God and walk in the spirit, not in the flesh. Did not Jesus proclaim, *"I am the way* [to live], *the truth* [reality], *and the life* [the victorious resource from which to draw]"? (Jn. 14:6) This is grace! This is *"grace abounding!"* And this is your testimony.

THE WORKING OF GRACE

A few years ago, the Lord came to me in the most unexpected way. One morning while I was driving, He spoke into my heart saying, "Would you like to be delivered from your addiction to TV?" Wow! I was almost too surprised to respond. "Yes, Lord," I replied. "You are free," He said. It happened, and for more than a year, I lived in this freedom. Over time, the tempter drew me back. I had a lot of time on my hands. Instead of occupying myself with the Bible, prayer and service, I began to watch the news channels, then other programs and sporting events, etc. I had fallen from grace in this area of my life. The victory in grace was there at every moment for me to seize, but I was neglecting to utilize it. By this I mean, that instead of enjoying Christ as my life, I was occupied with the world again in so many matters. I was not condemned to hell; rather, I had failed to remain in the freedom that grace had provided and supplied me. It sounds dumb doesn't it? Well, it is!

This kind of thing happens to Christians all the time. This is why the *"Spirit of grace"* (Heb. 10:29) comes to rescue us all the time. Accusation and condemnation descended upon me. I struggled with this for a period of time, but eventually I gave in to the TV. Again I was wasting hours watching news, sports, and favorite programs. I still enjoyed the Lord in many ways and was always in fellowship with other believers, but in this particular area I was being defeated. As far as TV was concerned, I was in the jaws of Romans chapter 7. My relationship with God became more casual than fervent. My concern for spiritual things cooled. The power in my witness was leaking away. Others may not have noticed, but I knew that there was little anointing in my speaking. People were no longer being changed by my service and preaching. I tried harder to improve but that had no benefit. I had fallen from grace. You want to know what happened don't you?

In 2 Thessalonians 1:11-12 Paul tells us,

> *"Therefore we also pray always for you that our God would count you worthy of the calling, and fulfill all the good pleasure of His goodness and the work of faith with power, that the name of our Lord Jesus Christ may be glorified in you, and you in Him, according to the grace of our God and the Lord Jesus Christ."*

It is so easy to stray from God. There is a lot of stuff and people programmed to help us Christians get derailed from the path of godliness. But as these two verses reveal, there are those who are praying for us. We know for sure that our Mediator in heaven (Jesus) is making intercession for us before God. We should not be surprised when God intervenes in our circumstances to save us.

Consider what kind of prayer Paul is praying for the Thessalonians. To be worthy of God's calling is to fulfill all the good pleasure of His goodness and the work of faith with power. God our Father has an irrevocable, good plan over all of His children. It is filled with His goodness and His work of faith with power. This operation is ongoing without interruption on His side. His divine operation will eventually elevate us into our transcendent destiny to live by the *"faith of the Son of God Who loved me and gave His life for me."* (Gal. 2:20)

Grace to abandon the TV was always present and available. However, this time it did not come to me instantly. This time I escaped the mesmerizing hold by consciously and deliberately choosing to be with God.

The divine communion occurred by means of meeting with other Christians, reading Christian books, meditating in the Bible, and prayer. The key word here is that I chose to be with God, not the distractions. On each occasion there was a defining moment wherein I made the choice regarding my direction, focus, and intensity. Nothing compares with the peace and tranquility of divine communion. Grace transmits heaven's benefits. The simple factor is one of preference not performance. Peter's words are riveting. When asked by the Lord if the disciple also wanted to desert Him, Peter said, *"To whom shall we go? You have the words of eternal life."* (Jn.6:68) Many who had been following Jesus found it hard to understand what He was teaching and left Him to pursue other things. Don't we at times forsake the living Word to seek the things of the world? Unfortunately, I admit I do. That is not a wise decision. Let's be honest with ourselves and each other here. Our daily life with its momentary decisions is where the action is. This is the battlefield on which the engagement is decided and the victory seized or forfeited. It is all about our choices. God made us free-willed people in order that our testimony would be the sum of our choices.

When Joshua brought the people of Israel across the Jordon River into the promised land of Canaan, he gathered the people together there. God spoke through Joshua to Israel with these words:

> *"Now therefore, fear the* LORD, *serve Him in sincerity and in truth, and put away the gods which your fathers served on the other side of the River*

and in Egypt. Serve the LORD*! And if it seems evil to you to serve the* LORD*, choose for yourselves this day whom you will serve, whether the gods which your fathers served that were on the other side of the River, or the gods of the Amorites, in whose land you dwell. But as for me and my house, we will serve the* LORD*."*

(Josh. 24:14-15)

Christ has won for us total victory, but our choice makes the application or not. Peter's response exemplified enlightenment and wisdom. *"Lord to whom shall we go? You have the words of eternal life."* (John 6:68) Peter was at the threshold of entering his journey of following Christ. Here, Peter was at the beginning of processing the things that render spiritual benefit. Now we and myriads before us are joining him by the choices we make by the power of the grace of God.

God's labor of salvation over us is so great and full of grace. We can live in a measure of glory now, and enter into His full glory at His coming. All through our life here on earth, the goal of God does not change, nor can it be derailed. We shall be changed! We are being saved by His life. You may ask how, but that is a subject too broad to cover here. Grace is God supplying Christ as our Savior to save us in all of our situations. I hope that we will let this sink down into our hearts with joy. By doing this, the name of our Lord Jesus Christ will be glorified in each of us, and we will be glorified in Him according to the grace of God. The result of all this shall erupt in a universal *"praise to the glory of His grace."* (Eph. 1:6) I trust that we all will learn to pray for one another like Paul did for the Thessalonians. Lord, help us in praying to pray with faith in God's outstanding grace.

Now listen to this story of what grace can do. *"But God, Who is rich in mercy for His great love wherein He loved us,"* (Eph. 2:4) was not far from me. Grace came! Jesus came to me again, but this time in the person of my family doctor.

My life was filled with a lot of circumstances. I had a heart condition, diabetes, a sizable financial loss, an aging mother, and a brother that was battling with cancer, etc. I was in Dr. H's office going through a routine exam. When I thought we were finished, the good doctor sat down in the corner and abruptly asked, "Are you depressed?" "No, I don't think so. I'm just going through some stuff." I lied! I was very depressed!

Hey, it is time to admit where we are and what we are doing in our living. Self deception and deceiving others is darkness and is from the evil one. I had one foot stuck in the world and was not exercising much effort to extract it. It is like running a red signal light and then excusing yourself. In some areas like the TV thing and allowing anxieties to overwhelm my emotions, I was not in the light of God. I needed to own up to the truth and face it with someone.

I further explained to the doctor in my religious language (which I hide behind sometimes when inhibited from being painfully transparent), how I was trying to rise above these nagging problems. He wasn't buying it! He pressed on. "Is it working?" I was "busted," and I knew it. It was time to quit hiding and deceiving myself. He may not have been ready for this, and for sure I was not. He walked over to the exam table, pulled up the back and began to write his analysis on the paper that covered the table. He gave me a prescription of truth as he saw it. Doc said, "You know what I see here in front of me? I don't see Herman; I see apathy! You are a fighter, Herman. This posturing is not you." Without being polite or politically correct, Doc was telling me to get back into the game and play like a winner.

There was no pity in his voice. He spoke firmly, directly to someone that he cared about. His attitude was not, "Get over it!" It was more like, "We're going to get through this together." This was the gospel according to the power of God. Though I was under the microscope of God, I needed to hear this. Dr. H was being constrained by the Spirit to speak directly to my heart. After a while, he walked back to his chair to sit down. I presumed that now he was done.

A few seconds of silence passed. I was too stunned and exposed in the light of that brief encounter to initiate anything or even get up. I was stuck in a three-way mediation. God was there with the doctor and me. God was winning. In a sense I wanted to dash out of that room, but I knew that some serious diagnosis was going on. I wanted to say something—anything to break the sobriety of the moment, but that wouldn't work either. Once more the grace of God took over as Dr. H said, "I am going to suggest that you read a book. You don't want to see the counselor I have recommended. You do not want more medication, so at least read this book." He wrote the title down on that oracle of paper from the exam table. It was not a book from the Bible or a spiritual book. The book was *Man's Search for Meaning* by Victor Frankel. This was an autobiography of a psychologist, a Jew who had been put into a concentration camp by the Germans during WWII. I got the book, and in those pages (page after page) I viewed the grace of God. This book is something of the outpouring of God's splendid operation of grace. After reading that book, peace and faith arose in me again. The problems were the same around me. But in the freedom of the grace that had come, I began to write this book. Isn't it surprising how God works in the most unexpected ways to deliver us?

THE GRACE GIVEN

As stated before, grace is for all of us! To each one of us grace is given! God is no respecter of persons. He plans for all of His children to *"grow"* in grace, be *"established"* in grace, and to *"reign"* in grace. Paul's greetings to the recipients of his letters read *"Grace to you and peace from God our Father and the Lord Jesus Christ."* This is not just a customary greeting. It is from the heart of one who knows the importance of grace experienced in the believer's daily life. In Ephesians 3:6-8 Paul says,

> *"…His promise of the gospel, of which I became a minister according to the gift of the grace of God given to me by the effective working of His power.*

*To me, who am less than the least of all the saints, this grace was **given**, that I should preach among the Gentiles the unsearchable riches of Christ."*

He goes on to say,

"But to each one of us grace was given according to the measure of Christ's gift."

(Eph. 4:7)

Abundant grace has been given to us by God. Don't get distracted by thoughts of unworthiness or supposed inadequacies. God is bountifully sending grace to enable us, yes, even you and me.

Quite a number of years ago, I began to make my habit to read through the Old Testament every year. During those years, I ran across a verse that nearly blew me away. While reading Proverbs, I got to chapter 22 and read,

"Incline your ear and hear the words of the wise,
And apply your heart to my knowledge;
For it is a pleasant thing if you keep them within
    you;
Let them all be fixed upon your lips,
So that your trust may be in the LORD;
I have instructed you today, even you.
Have I not written to you excellent things
Of counsels and knowledge,
That I may make you know the certainty of the
    words of truth,
That you may answer words of truth
To those who send to you?"

(Prov. 22:17-21)

I was not really alert because Proverbs is definitely not one of my favorite books. Suddenly, I sat up in my chair almost in shock. *"I have instructed you today, even you."* Do you know who Proverbs was written for? Do you know who the whole Bible was written for? *"You!"* That specifically means me! Read the verses again for yourself. What did you get? Well, that day I began to read the Bible like it was written and sent special delivery to me. My desire and habit is to read it with the understanding that everything God has done through His grace is for me. Yes, grace is for me—and you too.

Look, if you are a believer, you can receive a lot of grace. You and I are the object of God's grace. He is effectively and powerfully pouring as much grace into you as you allow Him to do. This grace saves us, delivers us, protects, and preserves us at all times and in everything. God's graciousness transcends adequate human language, yet we still endeavor to make it known. Peter put it this way,

> *"But you are a chosen generation, a royal priesthood, a holy nation, His own special people, that you may proclaim the praises of Him who called you out of darkness into His marvelous light."*

> (1 Pet. 2:9)

We believers have tasted grace in the salvation of God. We are joyfully trying to tell the story of the gospel of our salvation. Hear Paul's words again,

> *"Grace to you and peace from God our Father and the Lord Jesus Christ."*

> (Eph. 1:2)

God has not merely served up an appetizer. He has prepared an eternal feast of grace. Come and dine!

Paul considered himself the least of all saints because he formerly had been a destroyer of those who were of the faith. Nevertheless, Jesus pursued him to make him a believer and an apostle to the world. To this kind of man came the measure of the gift of Christ. Thus it is with each of us who have believed into Jesus. The effective working of God's power is in the grace we are daily enjoying. This is the nature, potential, and purpose of God's grace deployed to each of us to accomplish our salvation and to enable us in our service.

GRACE BESTOWED IN THE CHURCH

To the church in Ephesus Paul writes:

> *"But to each one of us grace was given according to the measure of Christ's gift. Therefore He says: 'When He ascended on high, He led captivity captive, and gave gifts to men.' …And He Himself gave some to be apostles, some prophets, some evangelists, and some pastors and teachers, for the equipping of the saints for the work of ministry, for the edifying of the body of Christ, till we all come to the unity of the faith and of the knowledge of the Son of God, to a perfect man, to the measure of the stature of the fullness of Christ; that we should no longer be children, tossed to and fro and carried about with every wind of doctrine, by the trickery of men, in the cunning craftiness of deceitful plotting, but,*

*speaking the truth in love, may grow up in all
things into Him who is the head—Christ—from
whom the whole body, joined and knit together by
what every joint supplies, according to the effective
working by which every part does its share, causes
growth of the body for the edifying of itself in love."*

(Eph. 4:7-8, 11-16)

Isn't it astonishing what the grace given to us can
do? The preceding portion in Ephesians is super packed
with the effective operation of grace in God's administration of building up His children in each local church.
Consider yourself as one of these very special children.
That is absolutely the way He views each one of us. You
and I are fully qualified to lay hold of as much grace as
anyone that has ever entered into the family of God.
There's something to think on!

When Jesus rose from the dead, He led captivity
captive and gave gifts to men. These *"gifts"* were people
who were called and specially anointed with particular
functions as identified above. These particular men and
women were commissioned to equip and facilitate all
other "saints" who directly build up the church in each
locality. However, let it be clearly understood that there
are no special or elite folks in the church of our Lord.
We all are equally His beloved.

Christ gives gifts to each saint and gives the apostles, prophets, etc. to help them develop in their specific
gifted function. The gifts Jesus gives us, His saints, are
far, far too numerous to name. That would be like trying
to name all the parts and functions of the human body
down to the cellular level. Yet, as many as there are, we

value each one of them. We are very unwilling to give up any member of our wonderful body. In the same manner, every son of God is indispensible in the body of Christ. Every believer is precious to Christ, and his function with his gift is not expendable.

The point of the verses quoted above is that we all may effectively learn how to use what God has given us. Just like an athlete, surgeon or musician develops his skills, we also must develop the gift God has given us. Have you discovered your gift? It is not that hard to do. It is not necessary for something dramatic to happen. No! No one has to come and lay hands on you. Your gift came with your new birth. Some believers do receive a special gifting by the laying on of hands or by prophecy. Timothy received a gift in that manner, but that is not how most receive their gift.

> *"Do not neglect the gift that is in you, which was given to you by prophecy with the laying on of the hands of the eldership."*

> (1 Tim. 4:14)

Not many believers, however, experience this kind of impartation. Our gifts come to us by the grace of Christ's giving.

We are endowed with our gift at the time we receive Christ as our Savior. He supplies more giftings as we need them in our service before Him. I hope that the simplicity of this will become a settled matter in your heart. The Holy Spirit will work within each of us according to the gifting of God in us. We will never lose our gift for the scripture tells us that *"the gifts and the calling of God are irrevocable."* (Rom. 11:29) You have what you need to serve God and the body of Christ, so discover it (if you haven't) and use it joyfully! By the way, we never get to retire from serving with this gift. We actually get more proficient in using it as we mature.

There are many Christians who function in their gifting for perhaps a number of years before they identify what it is. Think about the things that you do most often and easily. The gift that God has put in you is the thing that you spontaneously do in serving with others in the church. How about that? Some folks like to cook, so they take food to the sick, bereaved or needy members. Some folks serve by taking care of the practical needs of those who have been incapacitated by an illness or injury. They visit these people and clean the house or do the wash for them, etc. I have seen mechanically gifted brothers repair cars for others without charge. Some saints have purchased personal goods for families in need. I have seen some brothers and sisters buy appliances and cars for other members of the body of Christ who could not afford these items. Some minister in prayer for others. There are some who can pray for the sick, and the sick are healed. Some minister the Word of God, and the hearers are comforted. There are so many ways that the grace of God is ministered throughout the church.

This is indeed how grace works. It is God doing for you what you cannot do for yourself. The reason it is so spontaneous and remarkably easy is because God is operating through you. Think of the whole scope of human needs. Jesus desires to meet all these needs through the members of His body serving each other. This is the *"manifold"* grace of God that builds us up. The operation of these gifts in the brothers and sisters ministered in love causes praise and worship within us as we experience and observe it in the glorious body of Christ.

Here is another example. Some years ago a couple in our church had a baby that had chronic colic. Their doctor prescribed a drug that caused an addiction in the baby. The couple was told that it would take months to reverse this condition by slowly reducing the dosage given the child. When our brother shared this with his close friends in the church, a few brothers and sisters went over to his house that evening to pray for their baby. Within only a few moments of prayer, faith came to all of us, and the baby was instantly healed. What we could not do for ourselves, God did! That is grace in action.

Another example of God's gracious operation occurred in my life in 1963 while I was attending college at Baylor. My parents were not financially able to send me to college, so I was working my way through school each semester. At the beginning of my sophomore year, I was lacking the necessary funds to return to school. I had a little money saved from working full time, but it was not adequate. I was confident that God wanted me to go back to school, so I packed my belongings and prepared to leave on a Sunday afternoon. That Sunday morning the strangest thing happened. A postal jeep pulled up in front of my parents' home where I was living. The postman came to the door and handed me a special delivery letter which contained a check for $700. That considerably exceeded my need for the semester. The letter inside said that a member in a church in Dallas, Texas, had heard of me and wanted to help. I never found out who the donor was. What I could not do for myself, grace labored in someone to do for me. Can you imagine the praise and thanksgiving that we experienced that morning?

I would like to mention another example wherein my family experienced the abounding grace of God. In 1985 I became very ill as a result of chemicals that I came in contact with on a daily basis in my business. As a result, I had extreme memory loss and had to give up my business. For almost a year I lay in bed confused, disoriented, and very dependent on my wife and children. My wife was teaching in a junior high school; my son was a junior in high school; my daughter was in the eighth grade. I was not capable of doing much to take care of my needs because I couldn't remember what to do from hour to hour. While Kathleen was teaching she had to check on me several times a day to make sure that I had taken my medicines on time. If she did not call me to remind me to take them, I often would forget to do that. She would then need to call to make sure that I had taken them. Often, within five minutes after the scheduled time, I would not remember if I had taken my pills. It really was that bad. We had little revelation of Christ as the Healer during those years; consequently, we experienced healing very infrequently.

I also was put on a rotation diet which required that if I ate something in a certain food group I could not eat that item again for five days. The care that I required was extremely demanding upon Kathleen and the children. To make matters worse, I was not the best of patients. Often, I would be irritable and unpleasant. This charged the environment of our home with a lot of uncertainty. I felt totally useless and wondered if I would ever be able to work again or even be normal. Our church provided financial assistance through much of that time, an act of amazing grace! The children continued to do well in school. In fact, my son got an appointment to the Air Force Academy. My wife and daughter grew very close to each other during this adversity and still enjoy a deep love for each other today.

My recovery took almost five years. In spite of my problems, I still clung to my faith that God was in control. He would never abandon me. During that time I went back to college to get my teaching certificate brought up to date. Even with memory problems, I was able to maintain a 4.0 average for thirty-two hours of course work. That had not been the case in my undergraduate courses, ever! Is it not amazing what grace does when we allow God to be our Father of love and supply? Most of the time, we are never ready for this kind of suffering, but things like that happen to us all. The most remarkable thing is that it gives us opportunity to get to know the magnificence of our Father. He delights to meet us in our weakness and helplessness. That is how grace works.

Paul said it so well for all of us who know something of such abounding grace. Regarding his own experience he proclaimed,

"But by the grace of God I am what I am, and His grace toward me was not in vain; but I labored more abundantly than they all, yet not I, but the grace of God which was with me."

(1Cor. 15:10)

Take a few minutes each day to reflect on your own experiences of God's gracious involvement within your daily life. Isn't He faithful and reliable? I think I know your answer.

And here is a recent discovery of mine. While reading the book of Hebrews this last October, I noticed that even Jesus as a man required the grace of God. While He was in the garden of Gethsemane before the coming crucifixion, He was praying and seeking strength to undergo the coming trauma. As He was crying out to God, a wealth of grace was supplied to Him. Listen to this:

But we see Jesus, who was made a little lower than the angels, for the suffering of death crowned with glory and honor, that He, by the grace of God, might taste death for everyone.

(Heb. 2:9)

OBSERVING GRACE IN OTHERS

Many times I have observed couples in the church give themselves to invite people into their home for dinner and an evening of fellowship. This clearly exemplifies the "multiplied grace" which is given to people. To do this consistently for years and with equitable love for everyone seems somewhat beyond our human virtue. In these kinds of gatherings, their guests were always richly blessed and encouraged. Sometimes the host couple was not gifted in directing or leading the fellowship into Christ-centered conversation. But they always made sure that one of their guests had such ability. Around their table people learned the wonders of Jesus as Savior, the Author and Perfecter of faith, and many grew into maturity as a result of this kind of ministry. Some mature couples would counsel younger couples or single people in these kinds of home settings. I watched others commit to move families from one home to another after the sale or purchase of a new home. Sisters helped pack and unpack cabinets and clean the vacated home. On one occasion, a couple drove one of our two U-Haul trucks 1,000 miles to our new home in Oklahoma. Then they stayed with us a few days to help us clean and arrange things in our new home.

Recently a family in our local assembly with a newborn baby had their only car stolen. That brother called a church member with whom he had built up a relationship to explain what had happened. That evening a number of fellow believers arranged to loan them a car and an infant car seat. One family provided transportation for the brother back and forth to work for a few days. Others helped with meals and laundry.

This mutual assistance is not unusual in the body of Christ. Now, pause for a moment to think about what brings you a sense of satisfaction in serving others. This labor of love may seem simple and easy to you, but it may be beyond the ability of others. As you serve in the way you do, realize that it does not necessarily have to appear to be something "spiritual." When Jesus fed the multitudes, was that "spiritual" as we think of spiritual things? To my thinking, that was something very practical.

I have also observed that as saints love and serve each other, opportunities and giftings will increase. Perhaps this is one of the true meanings of what *"growing in grace"* is all about? Keep in mind that this grace is God in Christ overcoming every negative thing that has separated God from man. On the positive side, grace is God in Christ accomplishing everything that the Father had purposed that man should accomplish on earth. In a very proper sense, grace here is a synonym of Christ.

When you see fellow believers ministering like this, doesn't it cause an appreciation to arise in your heart? When you see someone doing something that results in benefit for another person, you are seeing grace in action. Once I realized that I was getting to observe God's grace flowing through people, I began to watch for it. As a result I was ushered into a realm of thanksgiving and praise that I had not known before. I was beginning to view the love and hand of God working in so many ways that I had overlooked before. This caused me to have greater expectations and faith that God was with us and doing many wonderful necessary things that people need. When we realize that grace is administered through the members of the body like this, our faith and appreciation of God as Father increases exponentially. This is exactly how Jesus came declaring the person and nature of God. He took care of people in their practical situation. That was the proof of the declaration of the apostle, John, who said that Jesus came full of grace. Now I find it extremely enjoyable to watch for grace working through others. So rather than discount the little things you do for others, having been prompted somehow, do it with the understanding that grace is working in you for others. It is the word of His grace operating in you to build up the church around you. And that is a beautiful thing—Christ in us the hope of glory!

GRACE FOR DAILY LIVING

I start this section with Taylor's story. My older brother has many stories of how God's grace brought him through a variety of situations. This one is particularly dear to me because it happened when he was very young. It stands out as a strong verification of the Lord's reassurance to Paul when He said, *"My strength is perfected in weakness."* (2 Cor. 12:9) Here is the story in Taylor's own words:

> After my junior year in high school, I felt like I needed to get away from home and strike out on my own. I went to work in East Texas at a truck stop. In the evenings, I pumped gas and changed truck tires. Quitting school and leaving home was a dumb thing to do, but I did it

anyway. In this small town, I found a widow lady that rented me a room with a bath. That part went well. I would eat at a Bar-B-Q place about noon, and they would pack me a sandwich for later on. That job at the truck stop lasted about four or five months.

There was a fellow who regularly traded at the station, and he was looking for someone to clear his wooded land. As I remember it was about 160 acres with the Sabine River running through it. After some friendly negotiations, I agreed to take on this job. I was seventeen years old and of course a very clever businessman. The gentleman told me that I could have all the wood I cut, live in his barn, and even use his old Chevy pickup. There was no way I was going to pass up this kind of life style. So I drove back to Dallas, went to an Army/Navy store, and bought me a twelve-by-fourteen foot wall tent. I picked up my dog at Mom's house and back to East Texas I went! I had cut and sold fire wood before when I was in junior high school, so I had some knowledge of what I was doing and what I needed. I definitely needed the dog.

This was the period of time that the Interstate System was beginning to be constructed in that area. A lot of the local folks were working on the right of way clearing trees for contractors. I met one of these guys, and he sold me his twenty-six inch Poland chain saw. Now I was in business.

The time that sticks out in my mind is when I cut down the biggest oak tree that I had seen that fall. It started one morning in November.

That morning was cool, and a light frost was on the ground as the sun came up. It was a quiet morning and not even a breeze was stirring. Now this oak tree was huge, and I was eager to get it on the ground.

I had cleared all the area around the big old oak, so there was plenty of room to cut up all the large limbs into fire wood. I don't remember the size of the trunk of that oak, but my twenty-six inch saw blade would not reach across the whole trunk. I figured that I would sorta "gnaw" my way around it. As I undertook this task, I failed to realize that there was not a proper angle on my cut. When I had cut nearly completely through the trunk, this tree just sat down on my saw. The saw was pinned down. I couldn't budge it at all.

I desperately began to push on that tree to shove it over. It didn't move. Then I got the idea to drive some wedges into the cut. The green wood and the moisture in the tree made this like putting a toothpick into butter. Everything I tried didn't amount to much. Can you visualize my predicament? Listen, I am a smart high school dropout.

The next idea was to tie a chain as high as I could reach around that oak. Then I tied the other end to the front of the truck. I am smart enough to know that if I tied it to the back bumper the tension would just lift the tires off the ground. That would at best give only a small jolt on the tree. I needed more than a jolt. The engine weight would keep my tires on the ground, and the back wheels would maintain their traction. Besides that I would be able to keep my eyes on the tree and watch this giant fall. Of course knowing nothing of engineering, that was about as far as my deep thinking went. Anyway, I had it all figured out.

Now try to believe this. With all the pulling and yanking I did, that old tree didn't even drop a leaf. That was probably a good thing. It hadn't occurred to me that if that monster did fall that it would have crushed the truck with its content. I don't know why I had not thought of that. I needed some more high school. I guess I thought I would outrun it when it started to fall. Boy was I dumb! That chain was not going to get any longer than its twenty feet; that was for sure. A few tries yielded no success. I gave up, unhooked the chain, and pulled the truck out of the way. I cut some bigger wedges and tried driving them into the saw cut. That didn't help either.

Here I was with my capital investment of one used Poland chain saw stuck in that giant oak. I knew nothing else to do but pray. "Lord, I need help!" Last resort? Yep! Why do we leave God out until we have tried everything else? I sat there on a stump, petted my dog, drank a cup of coffee, and waited for God to do something. You know what? Nothing happened. Probably what was going through my mind was something like this. When is the good Lord going to send help? Have you been there before? Maybe you have, just not at seventeen.

Now that my saw was not running anymore, there was only the stillness of the woods. Then it dawned on me that I could hear another chain saw running somewhere east of me. That meant that I was not alone that day in those woods. My dog and I jumped into that old Chevy. I was determined to find that other saw and its owners. From the sound, I could tell that it must be in an area where I could see a column of smoke rising into the air. Since there was not a breath of air moving, those guys had to be where that fire was burning. That smoke was going straight up and the buzzing of that saw was coming from that same area. I was getting excited. If I found the fire, I would find another chain saw, and cut my saw out of that stubborn oak. It made me think of the three wise men and a star. Follow the smoke!

Then, the saw stopped. But there was still the smoke. It took me about an hour to find that fire with its smoke. There were two men there sitting around the fire and taking a break from cutting the trees. I walked up to them and introduced myself. They had heard my saw and had wondered if I was the one living in the big tent. I explained everything to them. I told them about the trouble that I was in. I begged them to come rescue me and my saw. I think they agreed to help me because they were mostly curious about me, my dog, and that tent. What in the world was a kid doing out here in the woods by himself?

They loaded their gear up and followed me in their truck back to my camp. Are you ready for this? The shock of my life was before us. That great big old oak tree was not standing there anymore. It was lying on the ground right where I had wanted it to fall. The Poland saw was on the ground, undamaged, at the base of the tree.

My new friend said, "I thought you said that we needed to cut the tree down above your saw. Did someone else come cut this thing down?" It was obvious that there were no new cuts on the tree. My answer was simple. "No, no one else cut it down. God must have pushed it over for me!" Hey, there was no wind that day!

That is Taylor's early adventure into getting to know the grace that God delights to pour out onto His children. I love this story. I love God our Father who takes care of us, even when we may be out in the woods being goofy. These early experiences of grace surely helped prepare Taylor for challenges in his adult life, such as being a Marine in combat in Viet Nam. Can you relate to this? Recall the numerous times that God intervened in your life circumstance to rescue you when you could do nothing more for yourself. He is like that. God delights and longs to do this kind of thing for us every day. Will we learn this and let Him?

It is precisely here that so many of us "miss the mark" of allowing the rains of heaven's grace to saturate our souls. It seems to me that in our daily routine we do most of what we do out of habit. What we do is according to our manner of life, based on what we like, or find convenient, or what seems to encounter the least amount of resistance. Whether we are young or elderly, we have learned to do most of what we do by building up a habit as our manner of life. Is our manner of life one of walking in the Spirit and being led by the Spirit? There is a remarkable verse in 2 Timothy 3:10 which says, *"But you have carefully followed my doctrine, manner of life, purpose, faith, longsuffering, love, perseverance...."* In this verse Paul discloses his strategic way of life.

The Greek word "agoge," translated *"manner of life,"* is used only once in the New Testament. Paul uses it here to strongly encourage his son in the faith. He reminds Timothy that by living in the spirit and by the grace from God in every situation, he will prevail.

It is so meaningful to me that Paul selects this special word to place in this crucial passage to his beloved son in the faith. The church had entered into a state of decline. Timothy was still a young man, perhaps ministering in the church in Ephesus. He may have been withdrawing in timidity from ministry because of the esteemed reputation of some of the leading ministers. At any rate, he needed these admonishing and strengthening words from Paul:

> *"Let no one despise your youth, but be an example to the believers in word, in conduct, in love, in spirit, in faith, in purity. Till I come, give attention to reading, to exhortation, to doctrine... Take heed to yourself and to the doctrine. Continue in them, for in doing this you will save both yourself and those who hear you."*
>
> (1 Tim. 4:12-13; 16)

It seems that for whatever reason, Timothy had begun to withdraw from fully exercising his God-given gifts of grace in the church where he was. At this time Paul was in prison again. He writes to Timothy speaking of his *"manner of life"* in chapter 3. In a declining situation among the churches, Paul is calling attention to his personal lifestyle. He lived in the spirit and was constantly receiving grace from God to be what he was and to do what he did.

Timothy had paid attention to Paul's words of the previous letter and embraced them. Timothy had been strengthened to take care of his own manner of life, following in the steps of his mentor. He was reminded that it was in such a manner of life that Paul had been taught by the Lord Himself. Jesus Christ had ministered to Paul in every kind of circumstances and had delivered him out of them all. This was the labor of *"grace abounding."*

To be victorious in our living situations requires that we be established in grace and rooted and grounded in the Word of God. Paul's manner of life was filled with grace. 2 Corinthians 4:7-12 tells us his story:

> *"But we have this treasure in earthen vessels, that the excellence of the power may be of God and not of us. We are hard-pressed on every side, yet not crushed; we are perplexed, but not in despair; persecuted, but not forsaken; struck down, but not destroyed—always carrying about in the body the dying of the Lord Jesus, that the life of Jesus also may be manifested in our body. For we who live are always delivered to death for Jesus' sake, that the life of Jesus also may be manifested in our mortal body."*

Grace is marvelous in whatever way it reaches man. Its source is God, and its content is all that God has done or is doing to reach man to bring him into His divine purpose. The whole creation rests under the bounty of God's grace. The laws of nature are the result of His grace. Thus everyone and everything is the beneficiary of the *"manifold,"* grace of God. Do not think that only Christians get to experience this blessing. God makes his rain to fall on the just and unjust. There are perhaps myriads of unsaved people who have been healed by the graciousness of our Lord before they were saved. This is the manifestation of the outpoured love of God, the *"true grace of God in which we stand."* (1 Pet. 5:12). Thank You, Abba Father! Thank You for renewing and refreshing us with the moments of grace upon grace.

The apostle John tells us, *"And of His fullness we have all received, and grace for grace.* (Jn. 1:16) Whoever touches Jesus will experience grace upon grace. Again the picture of a river of grace comes to mind. At one moment the water before you is consistently replaced by new and equally refreshing water. Upstream, this water has already imparted its gift; downstream, it will continue to bless everything and everyone awaiting it. It never ends. It is exhaustless! Those who preceded us were in the upstream blessing. Now we are in the downstream blessing. All enjoy the same stream and nothing is lost in the flow.

In Ezekiel 47, there is a compelling example of this flowing river. Everywhere the river flowed there was an abundance of life. From its small beginning, at the threshold of the house of God, the flow increased until it was a large river, *"waters to swim in."* Its progress captures the man of God. Our beginnings may seem small, almost insignificant. But as we *"grow in grace and the full knowledge of our Lord and Savior, Jesus Christ,"* (2 Pet. 3:18) the level of grace within us will increase to the point of carrying us along in its life-imparting flow. Peter describes this as the *"grace of life"* that a husband and wife may experience together. (1 Pet. 3:7) My wife and I have grown together in this grace for forty-eight years, and we are witnesses to the reality of how powerful and reliable this grace has been to us. In the Ezekiel picture, on each side of the river and in the river was abundance of life. Life was produced everywhere the river flowed.

The metaphor in Ezekiel 47 portrays another picture of water. They are little pools of water. With these pools there was no flow. These pools probably were once part of the river's current, but now they are isolated and stagnant. Isn't this a lot like our life experience? Sometimes things related to our spiritual life just are not flowing. The current is completely undetectable. In times like these, when we feel like maybe God has disappeared, we need to reassure ourselves by the constant truth of God's Word. Don't let feelings or circumstances steal your faith and confidence that you are always in the hands of your heavenly Father. Nothing can snatch you out of His hands. Jesus promised that He was with us *"all the days, even to the end of the age."* (Matt. 28:20) We are not dead. We always can turn to Jesus and find grace that will restore the current of the waters again. He said,

"But whoever drinks of the water that I shall give him will never thirst. But the water that I shall give him will become in him a fountain of water springing up into everlasting life."

(John 4:14)

To drink the water is to spend time with Him. All spiritual reality and progress begins there with Him.

When we look heavenward and embrace Peter's exhortation to *"grow in grace,"* (2 Pet. 3:18) instantly we can get back into the current of grace. This is not hard to do. Reflecting on a few of the awesome times that the faithfulness of God has blessed you or rescued you will stimulate faith again. Just a few moments of contemplating the graciousness of God will reignite our joy, thankfulness, confidence and praise. The circumstance may not change, but you are changed. Your focus has changed from anxiety about circumstances to confident trust in your faithful and loving Father.

There are many dangers and pitfalls along our journey. Peter cautions,

"You therefore beloved, since you know this beforehand, beware lest you also fall from your own steadfastness, being led away with the error of the wicked."

(2 Pet. 3:17)

There is always resistance to the river's current. That is why it winds about here and there. In spite of all the resistance, it will make its way to its destiny. The grace that is coming presses the present grace on its way.

Nothing can stop it! And thus it is with our spiritual pursuit. With grace there is always its availability and supply for every human situation. Grace is the atmosphere of God in which we live. We can either embrace the grace given to live in its flow or live in the stagnant pools of yesterday's or last month's grace. The choice is ours. To grow in grace in the presence of resistance is the believer's other option. If we choose to take the way of grace, we advance with the operation of God. If we fail to take grace, we become like the "pools," and the result is not desirable.

CHAPTER 3

THE LABOR OF GRACE

In the preceding chapter, we focused on the daily life experiences of grace. Now let's look at what grace does. Grace labors! Often the Bible uses words and phrases that are not common to our culture's vernacular. That is because the God of glory is seeking to reveal that glory to His created centerpiece—man. To say *"grace labored"* is a grammatical personification. In Ephesians 3, Paul says that he had been shown the mystery of God. Indeed, God is mysterious to all mankind. For this reason Jesus and the New Testament writers often used metaphors, allegories, parables and pictures to draw back the curtains of divinity in order to help our understanding. In 1 Corinthians 15:10 Paul tells us, *"I labored more abundantly than they all, yet not I, but the grace of God which was with me."*

In essence it is very similar to what he says in Philippians 2:12-13, *"Work out your own salvation with fear and trembling; for it is God who works in you both to will and to do for His good pleasure."* The Father was

97

working through Jesus. Jesus is working through the Holy Spirit. Therefore, the triune God is working in us who believe. Consequently, it is God Himself who is operating in us to perform His administrative will as is described in Hebrews 13:20-21.

> *"Now may the God of peace who brought up our Lord Jesus from the dead...make you complete in every good work to do His will, working in you* [God is the operator here] *what is well pleasing in His sight, through Jesus Christ, to whom be glory forever and ever. Amen."*

Did you notice who the one working is? It is God Himself. The labor of the Father, Son, and Holy Spirit is personified in the *"word of His grace."* When we lay hold of this, the result will be a living in the same dimension that Paul described regarding his labor and ministry to present every man to God, full grown in Christ. *"To this end I also labor, striving according to His working which works in me mightily."* (Col. 1:29) He profoundly affirmed that it was God mightily operating within him. What a confirmation to Paul's words in 1 Cor. 15:10 of how it was the grace of God which was laboring in him. It is vitally imperative that we get this renewed understanding of the working of grace within our thinking. We don't work for God! By His grace, He is working in and through us by His glorious and mighty power. This revelation changes everything!

In the Old Testament, God was always seeking to perform His work on behalf of His people. That work primarily was outward and upon man's circumstances. It was almost completely outward and environmental.

Things changed dramatically in the New Testament. Now, God is intrinsically working through the God/man Jesus. John's gospel is inundated with expressions related to this new covenant reality. I spent a few months reading through the gospel of John just focusing on this major matter of the corporate co-laboring of the divine within the human—manifested in Jesus. The relationship Jesus and the Father enjoyed was a prototype of what our destiny is in this lifetime. Paul declares the same truth that God Himself was doing His work in Christ.

> *"Now all things are of God, who has reconciled us to Himself through Jesus Christ, and has given us the ministry of reconciliation, that is, that God was in Christ reconciling the world to Himself."*

> (2 Cor 5:18-19)

The way that God was working through Jesus Christ is the same way that He has designed to work through all of us.

The factor of grace operating within man cannot be overemphasized. As believers in Christ and sons of God, this is our newly created state of being. Grace occupies a prominent role in our development as sons of God. We need to recognize this labor of grace and yield to that labor. In this manner, we will fulfill God's plan in daily routine situations. Days spent with God in communion and cooperation with Him will be filled with joy and vitality. We begin to share in Christ's reigning authority. Mediocre will not describe any part of your life in Christ.

THE IMPACT OF GRACE

The impact of grace is described by Paul in Romans 8:2-3, *"For the law of the Spirit of life has freed me from the law of sin and death, for what the law could not do... God did."* What Jesus did as a man in perfect harmony with God, we may now experience by walking in the Spirit and not fulfilling the desires of the flesh. There is one requisite, however, to our entering into such a victorious relationship with God. We must set our mind on the spirit, not on the flesh. (Rom. 8:1,4) In Jesus, God comes to do His work within man and with the cooperation of man. This is what grace is all about, and this is grace working.

> *"God was in Christ reconciling the world to Himself."*
>
> (2 Cor. 5:19)

> *"Do you not know that Christ is in you?"*
>
> (2 Cor. 13:5)

> *"He breathed on them and said to them, 'Receive the Spirit.'"*
>
> (Jn. 20:22)

All of this activity of God engages man and impacts man's circumstantial life. By grace internalized, the divine integrates with the human. Much needs to be said about this, but that is somewhat beyond the parameters of this writing. In that matter, I commend you to the *"word of His grace which is able to build you up."* (Acts 20:32)

Can you imagine a world without God's grace operating in it? It would be chaotic. There was such a world in Noah's time. But God intervened and saved Noah's family and two of all the animals on the earth. That is the impact of God's grace. That should stretch anyone's imagination. If grace is multiplied in our time, would we not expect it to be even more spectacular? Grace comes to us as Christians in so many ways. Think about this for a few minutes. What would it be like without God's love, protection, keeping and healing power, or comfort? We are talking major impact—none of this available to anyone or anything. This would usher in a society of total chaos. Thank God, that is not our situation today!

Earlier I listed the transitive active verbs that occur with the word *"grace."* It is helpful to me to periodically review these verbs to be reminded, refreshed, and refocused by them. These verses trace the process of grace working, and the more I muse over them, the more the light of the glory of God seems to break upon my mind. In the letter to the Ephesians, Paul prayed twice for this to be the church's experience.

In chapter 1 Paul prayed,

"Therefore I also, after I heard of your faith in the Lord Jesus and your love for all the saints, do not cease to give thanks for you, making mention of you in my prayers: that the God of our Lord Jesus Christ, the Father of glory, may give to you the spirit of wisdom and revelation in the knowledge of Him, the eyes of your understanding being enlightened; that you may know what is the hope of His calling, what are the riches of the glory of His inheritance in the saints, and what is the exceeding greatness of His power toward us who believe, according to the working of His mighty power which He worked in Christ when He raised Him from the dead and seated Him at His right hand in the heavenly places, far above all principality and power and might and dominion, and every name that is named, not only in this age but also in that which is to come. And He put all things under His feet, and gave Him to be head over all things to the church, which is His body, the fullness of Him who fills all in all."

(Eph. 1:15-23)

To just read these verses is an exercise in itself. I hope that you read the preceding portion slowly and thoughtfully. The ground that Paul covers here about God's purpose for the believers is dimensionless. Everything that is spoken of in Paul's words here is the result of how grace impacts God and man. Similarly, in Ephesians 3:14-19, Paul said,

"For this reason I bow my knees to the Father of our Lord Jesus Christ, from whom the whole fam-

ily in heaven and earth is named, that He would grant you, according to the riches of His glory, to be strengthened with might through His Spirit in the inner man, that Christ may dwell in your hearts through faith; that you, being rooted and grounded in love, may be able to comprehend with all the saints what is the width and length and depth and height—to know the love of Christ which passes knowledge; that you may be filled with all the fullness of God."

I have been reading and meditating on these two prayers for over forty-five years, and they still challenge me in understanding the fullness of what Paul is petitioning of God for you and me! I have meditated over them; I have prayed over them, yet each new reading refreshes me as though it were the first time. These prayers are full of grace. It is my hope that you will be more enthralled than I am and be blessed beyond Paul's expectation when he made these petitions.

Dear saints, what Paul has said in the foregoing verses is operational in Christians today. A brother I know, whom we will call Thomas, retired from teaching in a special education position in the spring of 2010. One night in early December that year, he dreamed that one of the members of his former teaching group resigned. In the dream, Thomas saw that he went back to work taking her place. After he awoke, he was somewhat puzzled by the dream and decided to keep it in his memory.

Shortly after that, Thomas and his wife went to visit their son in Virginia over the Christmas holidays. After returning from their trip, our brother found a message on his home voice mail. It was from the school where he had formerly been employed. The person in his dream that had resigned actually had resigned, and the school district wanted Thomas to return to his old position. Brother Thomas accepted the position, knowing that he was being led by the Spirit of God's grace.

Ironically, one week after Thomas signed his contract, the district instituted a hiring freeze. This brother told me later that without the dream he probably would not have acted as quickly to investigate the position and would have missed this opportunity. Obviously, God was not through with the work He was doing with Thomas at that high school. What an example of *"grace upon grace."* This should be very common in our daily lives. When one is tuned in to the operation of grace, he will be led by the Spirit in what may seem extraordinary ways.

GRACE WARFARE

Our enemy the devil is constantly seeking to keep God's enlightenment from penetrating our mind.

> *"But even if our gospel is veiled, it is veiled to those who are perishing, whose minds the god of this age has blinded, who do not believe, lest the light of the gospel of the glory of Christ, who is the image of God, should shine on them."*

(2 Cor. 4:3-4)

Galatians 5:16 also tells us of this struggle,

"I say then: Walk in the Spirit, and you shall not fulfill the lust of the flesh. For the flesh lusts against the Spirit, and the Spirit against the flesh; and these are contrary to one another, so that you do not do the things that you wish. But if you are led by the Spirit, you are not under the law."

In the following verses in chapter 5, we read more of the details of this warfare.

"Now the works of the flesh are evident, which are: adultery, fornication, uncleanness, lewdness, idolatry, sorcery, hatred, contentions, jealousies, outbursts of wrath, selfish ambitions, dissensions, heresies, envy, murders, drunkenness, revelries, and the like; of which I tell you beforehand, just as I also told you in time past, that those who practice such things will not inherit the kingdom of God. But the fruit of the Spirit is love, joy, peace, long-suffering, kindness, goodness, faithfulness, gentleness, self-control. Against such there is no law. And those who are Christ's have crucified the flesh with its passions and desires. If we live in the Spirit, let us also walk in the Spirit."

(Gal. 5:19-25)

In this section Paul details the works of the flesh and the fruits of the Spirit. These are not merely contrasts. These are two realms. The old realm is the flesh with its works. The new realm is the Spirit with His fruits. Both realms are depicted with the consequences of living in them. Every Christian is engaged in the struggle between these two realms. It is an inward battle with outward consequences. Too often believers focus on the negative aspects of this war rather than on what is spoken about the Spirit. The Spirit is proactively warring against the flesh. Who wins? The answer is found in Romans 8 and Colossians 3. I quote them here:

> *"For the law of the Spirit of life in Christ Jesus has made me free from the law of sin and death."*

> (Rom. 8:2)

> *"Set your mind on things above, not on things on the earth. For you died, and your life is hidden with Christ in God. When Christ who is our life appears, then you also will appear with Him in glory."*

> (Col. 3:2-4)

I cannot resist inserting a small doctrinal comment here. This verse in Colossians does not mean that we have to strive to think about heaven all the time. That would be extremely burdensome. In my experience, I am learning that the more I spend time in fellowship with the Lord and the *"word of His grace,"* I find that I am more occupied in my mind with spiritual and heavenly matters. I pray more for the outflowing of God's purposes on earth and for specific manifestations of His love and power in all kinds of practical things. Let us take precautions not to get caught up in trying to fulfill some of the imperatives of the Bible apart from allowing grace to do its work in us. It really works better for me to receive the enablement that comes from above than to try to attain on my own the heavenly blessings.

You probably already knew this. I am so grateful that I am catching on along with you all.

Probably many of us are familiar with the Romans 7 conflict. There the natural religious man tries with the law of the mind to fulfill the Law of God. The result is frustration and failure. Romans chapter 7 concludes with the desperate cry,

> *"O wretched man that I am! Who will deliver me from this body of death?"*

> (Rom. 7:24)

Then Paul proclaims how to escape from this miserable condition. The secret is to set the mind on the spirit, not on the flesh. In Romans 8:5-6, Paul says,

> *"For those who are according to the flesh set their minds on the things of the flesh, but those who are according to the Spirit, the things of the Spirit. For the mind set on the flesh is death, but the mind set on the Spirit is life and peace."*

> (NASB)

Herein is the key to victory over the flesh. Christ is within the spirit of the believer. *"If Christ is in you, though the body is dead because of sin, yet the spirit* [your spirit and mine] *is alive because of righteousness,"* (Rom. 8:10). Because Christ is in our regenerated spirit, that is where the operation of grace resides and functions. As we set our mind on our spirit rather than the flesh, we allow the grace to flow into our soul, accomplishing the transmission of grace not only into us but also into our environment. Jesus is our life, strength, victory, and daily supply in our spirit. To go to our spirit is to commune with Jesus and allow His saving life to become our living victory. Now that seems like a workable plan. Thank you, Brother Paul, for making it so obvious for those of us who were not getting it.

The Bible declares,

> *"Inasmuch then as the children have partaken of flesh and blood, He Himself likewise shared in the same, that through death He might destroy him who had the power of death, that is, the devil, and release those who through fear of death were all their lifetime subject to bondage."*

(Heb. 2:14-15)

Let these verses occupy your mind for a few days. I am confident that you will never be the same. You will no longer be so vulnerable to the deceptions of the defeated devil. Occupy your thinking with the truth of having been released from the oppression and bondage of the one who has lied to you and stolen from you. Satan has sought to destroy your faith in God, and yes, even kill you. This verse boldly declares that Jesus has destroyed this deceiving enemy. When verses like these occupy our thinking, the Bible reassures us that we too are overcoming the evil one.

1 John 3:8 repeats this theme. *"For this purpose the Son of God was manifested, that He might destroy the works of the devil."* The stage now is set for grace to labor abundantly in us. Everything is accomplished on God's side. Now it is our turn to prove the things that are real.

This grace is like a tiger poised to take its prey. In grace is the kinetic energy of God along with all the myriads of the attributes that reside in Him Who sits on the *"throne of grace."* Paul, Peter, James, and John all enjoin, "grace to you" and "grace be with you" to their contemporary believers. Everything God has done through Christ is now in the Holy Spirit. This Spirit is now in us as the Word of His grace, all grace, true grace, His bestowed grace. This grace is Jesus enabling, empowering and blessing people everywhere. He wants to bless not only you and me, but also all the people we know and the people all around us. Let the tiger out!

CHAPTER 4

THE KNOWLEDGE OF GOD THROUGH GRACE

In the Old Testament, there are many verses that reveal the fact that God wanted to have a relationship with man in a very personal way. In Genesis He was walking and talking with Adam and Eve in the Garden of Eden. This must have been extremely pleasant for them all. As they walked and talked together, Adam was gaining knowledge of God. This is precisely why, when Satan came with his temptation, the bait was about knowledge, which supposedly was being withheld from them.

In the New Testament God does something so extraordinary that even the angels were in awe. God became a man. That night of the holy birth the angels were seen singing and praising God in a great anthem. God not only was going to redeem man, but He was going to display to all who saw Jesus what a God-man relationship was like. In so doing, Jesus was fulfilling the prophecy of Jeremiah which said,

> *"But this is the covenant that I will make with*
> *the house of Israel after those days, says the* LORD:

I will put My law in their minds, and write it on their hearts; and I will be their God, and they shall be My people. No more shall every man teach his neighbor, and every man his brother, saying, 'Know the LORD,*' for they all shall know Me, from the least of them to the greatest of them," says the* LORD. *"For I will forgive their iniquity, and their sin I will remember no more."*

(Jer. 31:33-34)

Jesus was the first man to live in this new dimension of total harmony with God. Jesus came to fully declare the Father. God had spoken through the patriarchs and prophets to Israel. Yet God was still quite mysterious to man. Hebrews 1:1-2 says, *"God, who at various times and in various ways spoke in time past to the fathers by the prophets, has in these last days spoken to us by His son."* God never intended that He remain a mystery to mankind. He desired that all men should come to a full knowledge of Him. That is why He sent Jesus to manifest Him as a man.

When Paul began his letters to the churches and to individuals, he characteristically spoke of the grace of God. When he closed his letters, he often mentioned the grace of God that was with the believers. In God's abundant and extended grace, He is supplying us with knowledge of Himself. This knowledge is called "truth" in the New Testament. Jesus is described by John as God coming into the world *"full of grace and truth."* The grace and truth that filled our Lord Jesus was for the specific purpose to reveal the person, attributes, and character of God to the world. Paul's mission as

an apostle of God was to unfold the hidden mystery
of God. The truth that Jesus said would set men free
was now being revealed to the world. Listen to Paul
describe his calling to do this.

> *"For this reason I, Paul, the prisoner of Christ Jesus
> for you Gentiles—if indeed you have heard of the
> dispensation of the grace of God which was given
> to me for you, how that by revelation He made
> known to me the mystery (as I have briefly written
> already, by which, when you read, you may under-
> stand my knowledge in the mystery of Christ),
> which in other ages was not made known to the
> sons of men, as it has now been revealed by the
> Spirit to His holy apostles and prophets: that the
> Gentiles should be fellow heirs of the same body and
> partakers of His promises in Christ through the
> gospel, of which I became a minister according to
> the gift of the grace of God given to me by the effec-
> tive working of His Power. To me who am less than
> the least of all saints, this grace was given, that I
> should preach among the Gentiles the unsearchable
> riches of Christ, and to make all see what is the fel-
> lowship of the mystery which from the beginning
> of the ages has been hidden in God who created all
> things through Jesus Christ; to the intent that now
> the manifold wisdom of God might be made known
> by the church to the principalities and powers in
> heavenly places, according to the eternal purpose
> which he accomplished in Christ Jesus our Lord."*

(Eph. 3:1-11)

Jesus Christ is now our mediator (priest) before
God. The function of His priestly service is to facilitate

the total relationship between God and man. Jesus as both God and man became such a priest (personally and exclusively) mediating in every transaction we have with God.

> *"Now this is the main point of the things we are saying: We have such a High Priest* [Jesus] *who is seated at the right hand of the throne of the Majesty in the heavens."*

(Heb. 8:1)

God's will is to be transmitted to man and through man. Today Jesus as our priest is transmitting that will directly to us. The object is to transform us from soul-driven and flesh-driven persons to spirit-centered persons and to conform us to the image of Christ. Paul proclaimed that his deep desire was that he might know Him, Jesus. Herein is the substance of our knowledge of God. It is the intrinsic, personal, intimate, and all-encompassing knowledge of God through Jesus Christ our Lord. In its fullness it is described by Isaiah who said,

> *"For the earth shall be full of the knowledge of the* Lord *as the waters cover the sea."*

(Isa. 11:9)

All of this is realized by grace operating as the *"Spirit of grace."*

The central mission of Jesus was hidden in God as a mystery. Christ came to reveal the mystery and in so doing, He would justify, reconcile, and redeem us.

In the New Testament, the Lord unveils this hidden purpose of God. He lived it and explained it to His disciples. God never intended for man to live in a state of ignorance about this mystery, which is declared by the Lord Jesus Himself. He spoke to the Father in prayer before His crucifixion saying,

> *"I have manifested Your name to the men whom You have given Me out of the world. They were Yours, You gave them to Me, and they have kept Your word. Now they have known that all things which You have given Me are from You. For I have given to them the words which You have given Me; and they have received them, and have known surely that I came forth from You; and they have believed that You sent Me."*

(Jn. 17:6-8)

This is also highlighted when Jesus was speaking to His disciples in the upper room that last evening before He was arrested and carried away to be crucified. (John 13-16) A part of that evening's fellowship went like this:

> *"Let not your heart be troubled; you believe in God, believe also in Me. In My Father's house are many mansions* [Gr. 'abodes']; *if it were not so, I would have told you. I go to prepare a place for you. And if I go and prepare a place for you, I will come again and receive you to Myself; that where I am, there you may be also. And where I go you know, and the way you know.*
>
> *Thomas said to Him, 'Lord, we do not know where You are going, and how can we know the*

way?' Jesus said to him, 'I am the way, the truth, and the life. No one comes to the Father except through Me. If you had known Me, you would have known My Father also; and from now on you know Him and have seen Him. Philip said to Him, 'Lord, show us the Father, and it is sufficient for us.' Jesus said to him, 'Have I been with you so long, and yet you have not known Me, Philip? He who has seen Me has seen the Father; so how can you say, "Show us the Father"? Do you not believe that I am in the Father, and the Father in Me? The words that I speak to you I do not speak on My own authority; but the Father who dwells in Me does the works. Believe Me that I am in the Father and the Father in Me, or else believe Me for the sake of the works themselves...

*If you love Me, keep My commandments. And I will pray the Father, and He will give you another Helper, that He may abide with you forever—the Spirit of truth, whom the world cannot receive, because it neither sees Him nor knows Him; but you know Him, for He dwells with you and will be **in** you. I will not leave you orphans; I will come to you. A little while longer and the world will see Me no more, but you will see Me. Because I live, you will live also. At that day you will know that I am in My Father and you in Me, and I in you."*

(Jn. 14:1-11, 15-20)

In this passage, Jesus uses the word *"know"* or *"known"* eleven times. Consider the inseparable relationship that the Son has with the Father. In this discourse Jesus is clearly revealing the mystery of God for man, *"the mystery that had been hidden from ages."* (Col. 1:26) That mystery is that Jesus, now as the Holy Spirit who is called the *"Spirit of truth"* would come into His believers and be their life. To know God through Jesus as the indwelling Spirit of truth is the eternal mystery. This is the crowning work of grace. God and man are eternally joined together as one in life and nature. Paul makes this emphatically clear saying, *"He that is joined to the Lord is one spirit."* (1 Cor. 6:17) Peter confirms this declaring,

> *"To those who have obtained like precious faith with us by the righteousness of our God and Savior Jesus Christ: Grace and peace be multiplied to you in the knowledge of God and of Jesus our Lord, as His divine power has given to us all things that pertain to life and godliness, through the knowledge of Him who called us by glory and virtue, by which have been given to us exceedingly great and precious promises, that through these you may be partakers of the divine nature, having escaped the corruption that is in the world through lust."*

(2 Pet. 1:1-4)

I hope you noticed when reading John 17:6-8 that knowledge precedes believing. This is why the matter of actually knowing God is emphasized so much in the New Testament. This is the force behind Paul's words in Romans 10 when he says,

> *"How then shall they call on Him in whom they have not believed? And how shall they believe in Him of whom they have not heard? And how shall*

they hear without a preacher? And how shall they preach unless they are sent? As it is written: 'How beautiful are the feet of those who preach the gospel of peace, who bring glad tidings of good things!'

(Rom. 10:14-15)

For the Christian pilgrimage, there must be a beginning knowledge and a progressive knowledge, which flows into the full knowledge of God. Don't you have to admire the way God has planned everything and laid it out for us in Jesus Christ? For this to happen, grace is a key component.

THE TEACHING BY GRACE

Grace is our teacher.

"For the grace of God that brings salvation has appeared to all men, teaching us that, denying ungodliness and worldly lusts, we should live soberly, righteously, and godly in the present age."

(Titus 2:11-12)

Inasmuch as we have received more grace, we are taught by grace to know a variety of things. Just as the Holy Spirit is commissioned to teach us, so also the *Spirit of Grace* executes the same responsibility. In the preceding verse grace is teaching both negatively and positively. On the negative side, grace exposes the ungodly things and worldly desires. What grace is revealing related to these negative things is primarily perceived by us through our conscience. It most often is identified as an inner sensation of discomfort or uneasiness deep within. When we pay attention to this feeling and obey, we are being taught by the Spirit to avoid something that does not issue in our progress in living Christ's life. If we ignore that feeling, it gradually becomes less discernible over time. These are things that are destructive to normal Christian development. On the positive side, grace is instructing us to live soberly, righteously, and godly in the present age. Heeding what grace is teaching us results in living in the presence of God. The sensation that we experience when we obey the teaching of the Spirit of grace is one of light, peace, joy, satisfaction, and gratitude. This identification and obedience to the teaching of grace brings us progressively into a walk in the Spirit and in the presence of God. To live in His presence and in God's house is to be continually cared for by God's divine mode. In Psalm 36:7-9 we read:

> *"How precious is Your loving-kindness, O God!*
> *Therefore the children of men put their trust under*
> *the shadow of Your wings.*
> *They are abundantly satisfied with the fullness of*
> *Your house,*
> *And You give them drink from the river of Your*
> *pleasures.*
> *For with You is the fountain of life;*
> *In Your light we see light."*

This psalm describes the security of those who have put their trust in God. God is their provider and their safety. God is their satisfaction, and He is their illuminator. These believers have learned through time and experience that God is reliable for everything. God our Father, is always working in our circumstances to disclose His faithfulness to guard, supply, sustain, and enlighten us at the level Psalm 36 describes. Grace is very much a part of the divine instruction that will guide us there. Remember in Titus 2:12, grace is teaching us that *"we should live soberly, righteously, and godly in the present age."* This is a mirror of the Psalm 36 theme. Those who have been well taught by such amazing grace have learned to put their full confidence in God.

One song that I love has the following stanza which resonates the worship of Psalm 36:

> Grace in its highest definition is,
> God in the Son to be enjoyed by us;
> It is not only something done or giv'n
> But God Himself our portion glorious.

(Hymns,
Living Stream Ministry, Anaheim, CA, 1966)

Muse on the words of this hymn—"God in the Son to be enjoyed by us." As we enjoy the grace of God, grace is revealing God to us. Grace is teaching us things we cannot know apart from divine assistance. Doesn't this sound like the harmonious inner relationship that Jesus was describing to His disciples in John 14? Grace has now become our teacher even as the Holy Spirit is our teacher.

Paul is one who had learned to trust in the teaching of grace. In his letter to the Ephesians, he penned the key by saying, *"But you have not so learned Christ, if indeed you have heard Him and have been taught by Him, as the truth is in Jesus."* (Eph. 4:20-21) *"Heard Him"* and *"taught by Him"* are indeed phrases revealing the path of our upward progress into God's full salvation. When Paul was meeting with the elders of the church in Ephesus (recorded in Acts 20), he knew that he would not see them again. Somehow he also knew that serious problems lay ahead for the church there. Yet he comforted them in the following way.

> *"So now, brethren, I commend you to God and to the word of His grace, which is able to build you up and give you an inheritance among all those who are sanctified."*

(Acts 20:32)

This is one of the most powerful statements of faith recorded in the New Testament. Paul could commend the leaders of the church to the *"word of His grace"* with full confidence that God was backing him up. The grace that had been Paul's teacher was the same grace that the church in Ephesus could rely upon. We who many years later are passing through our trials have access to the same *"word of His grace."* By the teaching of this word of grace we all who have believed into Jesus shall be built up into the heritage of God. Grace here is conveying the *word* of God that is described in Isaiah 55:10-11 in the following way.

> *For as the rain comes down, and the snow from heaven,*
> *And do not return there,*
> *But water the earth,*

And make it bring forth and bud,
That it may give seed to the sower
And bread to the eater,
So shall My word be that goes forth from My
   mouth;
It shall not return to Me void,
But it shall accomplish what I please,
And it shall prosper in the thing for which I sent it.

This is what God says about His word. He sends His word indiscriminately for the blessing of all who live on earth. As the rains water the earth and make it bud, so the word of His grace will cause us to grow in Christ. God does not send His word in vain. It will accomplish what God sends it to do. In Jeremiah 1:12 we read: *"…I am ready to perform My word."* Isn't this powerful? God is always ready to perform His word. This should reassure every Christian heart every day in every human situation. Our Father in heaven is absolutely confident that His word will accomplish exactly what He sends it to accomplish.

Paul was equally confident about the effectiveness of the word which was being conveyed through grace to the believers. It surely had been effectively working in his personal ministry. Look at the manifestation of this in Acts 14:3. *"Therefore they* [Paul and Barnabas] *stayed there a long time, speaking boldly in the Lord, who was bearing witness to the word of His grace, granting signs and wonders to be done by their hands."*

Jesus also affirms the powerful operation of the word.

"Most assuredly, I say to you, he who hears My word and believes in Him who sent Me has everlasting life, and shall not come into judgment, but has passed from death into life."

(Jn. 5:24)

To pass from death to life is not a temporary thing. Neither is it simply a future event that will happen to us after we die. Passing into life out of death is constantly occurring in our Christian experiences under the teaching of grace. The goal of the teaching of grace is to lead us into godly living in this present world. Do we effectively realize that in every moment of our life, in every situation, the word of God's grace is with us? Do we let grace teach us in the moment?

The word is ready to accomplish in us and in our life situation what God has sent it to do! Let us lay hold of the living word of God in our moments. Thus we are continually passing into godly living in all our affairs. The result in each of our personal experiences will be the fulfillment of the words of Jesus in John 8:31-32. *"If you abide in My word, you are My disciples indeed. And you shall know the truth, and the truth shall make you free."* I am confident that today many, many more Christians are experiencing the impact of the teaching of the word of His grace. The resulting manifestation radiates the glory of God and is being seen in the faces of believers all over the world. You and I are called to be among these people who are living in this dimension of the gospel.

I met one such person in my youth. Mrs. Pearl Goode is her real name. She was known by many as Billy Graham's "prayer warrior." I met her at a Navigator meeting at the University of Maryland in 1964. She was an elderly lady with a fascinating relationship with God. When Pearl heard Billy Graham preaching in his early evangelistic meetings, she was called by the Spirit to pray for his gospel campaigns. She took this ministry of prayer seriously and diligently. After some time of ministering in prayer for Billy, she began to go to the cities where he had scheduled a crusade. Weeks before the team was to arrive, she would spend days in prayer for that city and the lost that were to be saved. She would even go to the stadium or coliseum and move from seat to seat to pray for the person who would occupy that seat. She had an incredible walk with Jesus Christ.

On the evening I was privileged to hear her speak, she told the following story. She had been having some problems with her heart. During this time she was flying from one city to another and the plane began to pass through a thunderstorm. The plane was hitting pockets of strong turbulence and would suddenly drop significantly. If you have ridden a rollercoaster, you know the feeling.

Pearl was experiencing a considerable amount of discomfort. She lifted her Bible up into the air and shouted, "Lord, You know my heart can't take this. You get it stopped right now!" Immediately, the weather calmed, and the remainder of the trip was pleasant. Pearl said that shortly after the ride smoothed out, one of the stewardesses came to her and whispered, "Ma'am, you sure do enjoy your religion, don't you?" Of course we all laughed heartily. Yet the point was etched into my heart. God was with her in a dynamic way.

Pearl had walked with the Lord and had been taught by a daily living in His presence that she could exercise His authority just like Jesus did. Grace had taught her this. By receiving continuous supplies of grace, she knew Jesus, and she knew who she was in Jesus. This knowledge is for all of us to experience and employ!

After that meeting I walked out with her to the car. Within a few minutes of our conversation, I realized that this lady was "for real." Pearl Goode absolutely lived with Jesus! The Spirit of grace had taught her to rely on God in all of her circumstances.

While waiting for her driver, Pearl and I had a few minutes alone. She took me by the arm, looked me straight in the eyes and asked, "Young man, have you ever spent the whole night talking with God?" "No Ma'am," I said. "Well, tonight you go out there and do that!" said Pearl. Somehow I knew that was not a suggestion. So I did! That was a night I shall never forget. The impact of getting to know God like that has been inspiring my walk up to this day.

Over the next three years, I was blessed to visit with Pearl in her home a few times. She would always greet me warmly and invite me to join her. She didn't talk much at all. She would always invite me to pray with her. She didn't pray with her head down or anything like that. She prayed as she walked around her small apartment doing her chores, stopping now and then to encourage me to keep praying. She always prayed out loud and told me to do the same. Once she had gone into the kitchen during this prayer visit with Jesus, and I was left alone praying in the living room. Apparently I had paused longer than she thought necessary, and she thundered out, "Don't stop talking to Jesus, young man!" It has been forty-six years since that day, but still I can clearly hear that godly admonition. The grace that worked in Pearl began to work in me! By such wonderful grace, I am still being taught to know and enjoy the *"unsearchable riches of Christ."* (Eph. 3:8)

Today, we Christians know a lot about religious things such as rituals, traditions, ceremonies, and doctrines. The imperative thing that we need to know is—how well do we know God our Father and Jesus Christ whom He has sent? How frequently do I distinguish His voice from all others and obey Him? These thoughts are not introspective. I want to know and walk in the reality of who I am in Jesus and who Jesus is in me. Don't you? Paul and thousands of Christians have entered into the saving grace of His presence like this. Grace has taught them to live in the presence and authority of God.

THE GRACE FROM OUR FATHER

Now let's look at a few verses from the New Testament about getting to know our Father. Let's start with this one.

> *"Peter, an apostle of Jesus Christ, to the pilgrims of the Dispersion in Pontus, Galatia, Cappadocia, Asia, and Bithynia, elect according to the foreknowledge of God the Father, in sanctification of the Spirit, for obedience and sprinkling of the blood of Jesus Christ: Grace to you and peace be multiplied."*

(1 Pet. 1:1-2)

Perhaps all of us who have read the gospels have learned to appreciate Peter. He was bold, aggressive, and quick to state his opinion. He seemed to goof up rather frequently, and that is something I can relate to. But here in the verse above he is older, wiser, and calmer. He has become acquainted with God as his Father. In the introduction of this letter, Peter gives us a glimpse of what brought the change in his life. It is the multiplied experience of grace and peace. Grace brought him understanding, and peace was the result.

Peter goes on to say,

> *"As each one has received a gift, minister it to one another, as good stewards of the manifold grace of God. If anyone speaks, let him speak as the oracles of God. If anyone ministers, let him do it as with the ability which God supplies, that in all things God may be glorified through Jesus Christ, to whom belong the glory and the dominion forever and ever. Amen."*

(1 Pet. 4:10-11)

What happened to the bold bombastic Peter that too often started speaking before much forethought?

Grace had greatly impacted his manner of life. Isn't it interesting how frequently grace strategically appears in verses like this? It seems that it is out of the *"manifold grace"* that we have the ability and resources to live and serve one another. That is what changed brother Peter. The Spirit of grace is bringing us to God in order that we too may know Him in life transforming ways. The better we engage in the process of knowing our Father, the more we spontaneously experience Him and express Him to others.

"Grace and peace be multiplied to you in the knowledge of God and of Jesus our Lord." (2 Pet. 1:2) Here grace is multiplying in us to bring us into a peaceful relationship with God. By this grace we are getting to know our heavenly Father. However, it is vitally important to understand that we cannot be passive in this relationship. A few years ago I made a shocking discovery. As I was studying Hebrews 12:28, I noticed something that was particularly riveting to my mind. The verse says, *"Therefore, since we are receiving a kingdom which cannot be shaken, let us have grace, by which we may serve God acceptably with reverence and godly fear."* I noticed that the verb *"have"* [which in English grammar is passive voice] was in the active voice in the Greek text. Therefore it is not passive in the sense that we are waiting for grace to come to us. This means that we may definitely get very proactive about this. It literally means "to take grace." You and I may now exercise strong initiative in how much grace we activate in our soul. In the light of this, consider James 4:6-8,

"But He gives more grace. Therefore He says: 'God resists the proud, but gives grace to the humble. Therefore submit to God. Resist the devil and he will flee from you. Draw near to God and He will draw near to you."

In the beginning of this admonition, God is taking the lead to provide. Then we are commanded to join in. Since God has acted in our behalf, we have opportunity to respond in like manner with vigor!

In these three verses, consider the verbs gives, resists, gives, submit, resist, draw, and draw respectively are all in the active voice. Nothing is passive in these extraordinarily instructive, pertinent verses. God and we are to take action! In all this action grace is the center piece. Think about it! Our Father has supplied *"all grace"* to us. He makes it instantly available in order that you and I can lay hold of it! Let's take grace now! Let's apply this grace to everything and everybody around us.

God purposes that we know Him and understand how He is processing things in our lives. Be assured, however, that it has nothing to do with our own worthiness or effort. Listen, no one is more qualified to receive grace than another person. Everyone is equally designated as God's beneficiary of grace. The source is God! The substance is His victorious work in Jesus, and everything is being supplied through grace. What do we do? We pursue; we lay hold; we draw near to God who is lavishing grace upon us. It is in and by grace we draw near, submit and resist the devil. I reiterate, "God our Father is supplying all the grace that is needed for all the situations we face. Our Father is the supplier of grace; He is the source, and grace is the substance, the reality of everything that has been done for us in Jesus. Paul labored diligently to bring the saints to this kind of understanding of God. He said,

> *"For this reason I, Paul, the prisoner of Christ Jesus for you Gentiles—if indeed you have heard of the dispensation of the grace of God which was given to me for you, how that by revelation He made known to me the mystery (as I have briefly written already, by which, when you read, you may understand my knowledge in the mystery of Christ)."*

(Eph. 3:1-4)

Wow! Here again is the connection of grace and our personal knowledge and experience of God. It seems to me that the dispensing of the grace that Paul is referring to is for us to encounter grace in a way that unveils the mystery in a personal, energizing experience. Knowledge in itself is imperfect, but knowing God through experiencing grace is fulfilling and life changing. This is dynamic, kinetic Christian faith, not "church-going" tradition with no power. What is your preference?

The knowledge that Paul lived in and what he is beseeching his fellow believers to experience is found in 2 Corinthians 10:3-6.

> *"For though we walk in the flesh, we do not war according to the flesh. For the weapons of our warfare are not carnal but mighty in God for pulling down strongholds, casting down arguments and every high thing that exalts itself against the*

> *knowledge of God, bringing every thought into*
> *captivity to the obedience of Christ, and being*
> *ready to punish all disobedience when your obedi-*
> *ence is fulfilled."*

This is radical! Look at the bold proclamation of faith here. God has supplied grace, and Paul urges us to participate with responding boldness and courage. Paul's knowledge was one of clear discernment of what was of God and what was contending with God. There are fleshly things in our mind that we must recognize and reject by the authority of the Holy Spirit. Apart from grace we will never know the difference. When we lay hold of the gift of grace, we know God and flow with God in all things. Satan's strategy is to attack, accuse, confuse, deceive, and contradict the truth of Christ in the mind of all believers. That is how he endeavors to distract us from getting to know God effectively.

To the Philippians believers Paul describes his counter offensive to the diabolical plans of the devil to prevent him from knowing God,

> *"But what things were gain to me, these I have*
> *counted loss for Christ. Yet indeed I also count all*
> *things loss for the excellence of the knowledge of*
> *Christ Jesus my Lord, for whom I have suffered the*
> *loss of all things, and count them as rubbish, that I*
> *may gain Christ and be found in Him, not having*
> *my own righteousness, which is from the law, but*
> *that which is through faith in Christ, the right-*
> *eousness which is from God by faith; that I may*
> *know Him...."*

(Phil. 3:7-9)

Paul knew the secret and the mystery of God. He was committed to it as one discipled by Christ. The result was that the knowledge he had received from God became reality to him. Daily he intensely committed to be integrated into God's grace. This portion of scripture has enlightened and inspired countless thousands of Christians to pursue the person of Christ in the same manner. Look at the things in Paul's prayer for the brothers and sisters in the church at Colossae. He exhibits the deep desire of God for intimate communion with His family.

> *"For this reason we also, since the day we heard it, do not cease to pray for you, and to ask that you may be filled with the knowledge of His will in all wisdom and spiritual understanding; that you may walk worthy of the Lord, fully pleasing Him, being fruitful in every good work and increasing in the knowledge of God; strengthened with all might, according to His glorious power, for all patience and longsuffering with joy; giving thanks to the Father who has qualified us to be partakers of the inheritance of the saints in the light."*

(Col. 1:9-12)

As we fill our consciousness with God and embrace His words, we increase in our intimate knowledge of Him. Thus we are strengthened into God's power and authority. We interact with God in an inward knowledge of His will with all spiritual wisdom and understanding. Now that is both attractive and compelling.

Peter charges all of us to *"Grow in the grace and knowledge of our Lord and Savior Jesus Christ"* (2 Pet.

3:18). As we grow in grace and knowledge of our Lord, our hearts will *"...be encouraged, being knit together in love, and attaining to all riches of the full assurance of understanding, to the knowledge of the mystery of God, both of the Father and of Christ, in whom are hidden all the treasures of wisdom and knowledge"* (Col. 2:2-3).

I am so thankful that when Paul greeted the Colossian church that he did not say, "I am glad that you heard about Jesus and that you know about Him now." Paul's joy was altogether different than that kind of superficial comprehension. What he rejoiced in over these saints was something inward and life changing. He said,

> *"We give thanks to the God and Father of our Lord Jesus Christ, praying always for you, since we heard of your faith in Christ Jesus and of your love for all the saints; because of the hope which is laid up for you in heaven, of which you heard before in the word of the truth of the gospel, which has come to you, as it has also in all the world, and is bringing forth fruit, as it is also among you since the day you heard and knew the grace of God in truth."*

(Col. 1:3-6)

What does it mean to know the grace of God in truth? It means that we receive the benefits that grace supplies and utilize them. Imagine what God wants to do for you. While you are imagining that, realize that your heavenly Father is fully able to perform far beyond what you ask or think. Think about the revelation in the lives of these people who had formerly been Gentiles without God and without hope in this world. They were transported into another kind of living. They were entering into a direct knowledge and a personal relationship with God. The same is true of us today. This kind of knowledge has brought us into a 180 degree turn from darkness to light! Perhaps this is our highest expression of worship. We take the grace Abba is supplying, thereby displaying the Christ who lives in us and in whom we live and move and have our being. To live in grace is to worship God. Its destiny is to be harmonized completely with Him. Our grateful testimony will proclaim, *"and we beheld His glory, the glory of the only begotten of the Father, full of grace and truth."*

CHAPTER 5

GOD, YOU, AND GRACE

My overshadowing goal in this book is to elevate in your understanding the blessed part that grace is playing in the growth and perfection of your life with Christ. If our Christian progress is steady, we will currently taste of the *"good word of God and the powers of the age to come"* (Heb. 6:5).

> *"For in Him we live and move and have our being."*
>
> (Acts 17:28)

God surely has done everything on His side to *"save to the uttermost those who come to God through Him, since He always lives to make intercession for them"* (Heb. 7:25). God is the *"God of all grace, who called us to His eternal glory by Christ Jesus"* (1 Pet. 5:10). It is by His grace that God makes faith and love available to each one of us as an environment in which to live our Christian life.

"And the grace of our Lord was exceedingly abundant, with faith and love which are in Christ Jesus."

(1Tim. 1:14)

By His grace we have been *elected* (Rom. 11:5), *called* (Gal. 1:15), *justified* (Rom. 3:24), and *saved* (Eph. 2:5, 8). And by His grace we will be *glorified* (2 Thess. 1:12). In order to accomplish this, our Father *"according to the riches of His grace which He made to abound toward us"* (Eph. 1:7-8) has endowed us with grace flowing like a river.

On the cross Jesus said, *"It is finished"* (Jn. 19:30). Now, our Father wants to lavish this finished work of His grace upon us. As we pointed out before, *"Where sin abounded, grace has super abounded."* Jesus said,

"Whoever drinks of the water that I shall give him will never thirst. But the water that I shall give him will become in him a fountain of water springing up into everlasting life."

(Jn. 4:14)

Picture that in your mind. There is power in that springing up. There is constant nourishment and refreshment there. This water will produce an abundance of life and satisfaction. There can be no question about the adequacy and reliability of the salvation that God has accomplished for us. Draw near to Him and hear Him say it to you so personally, *"It is finished."* To think otherwise is to challenge the integrity and fidelity of God.

"And God is able to make all grace abound toward you, that you, always having all sufficiency in all things, may have abundance for every good work."

(2 Cor. 9:8)

Here is a verse that I pray that God would deeply inscribe into my heart and consciousness. God is able! *"Of course He is,"* you might say. I agree. So tell me now, can you honestly think of any reason that would hinder you from living today in the authority of all that grace supplies?

God is omnipotent! As I grow into a living faith, I confess that there is so much about my God and Father that I need to understand in order to magnify and glorify Him. On our side there still is much to be fulfilled in us. The Bible declares that Jesus *"is also able to save to the uttermost those who come to God through Him, since He always lives to make intercession for them."* (Heb. 7:25) Let us be absolutely assured; God is able, and Jesus Christ is able! We are in this laboratory of life to prove that. The goal of God is to save us completely. He is committed to this. He is reliable! However, we must ask, "What about our side—our cooperation?"

To the Ephesians, Paul said that grace was the gift of God. We all know that a gift is not earned. It is passed on to us through the benevolence of the giver. In our religious culture, how frequently do we hear things like the following? "Oh, I need to pray more." "I need to go to church more often." "I need to read the Bible more." "I need to memorize more of the Bible." "I need to visit the sick and needy in our church." "If I only tithed more faithfully…." Perhaps you do need to do these things, especially if the Lord is speaking about this to you. If He speaks to you like this, He will be the enabler to do it in you with joy. All of these things can be helpful and perhaps will result in healthy Christian growth. But deep in my own heart there is a nagging uneasiness—why am I thinking about improving in this way? How much do I really know the Truth that sets me free? Is there still some residual contemplation of establishing a measure of righteousness of my own that will convince God to be inclined to do something special for me? This is foolish thinking and a waste of energy. By His grace, let's cut this babble and direct our thoughts into the aspirations of God.

The gift of God is a gift. To do anything other than to receive it with thanksgiving and humility insults the Giver. Yet there is so much human effort driving most Christian organizations and denominations, and yes, most Christians. Is God stingy? Is He partial? Does He need our assistance? Do His resources run low at times? This mire of Christlessness inundates our current theology and Christian philosophy. Why? Because we have been poisoned by a deceiver who wants to make our Father of grace and salvation seem distant, unreliable, harsh and austere. Nothing is further from the truth. Let us repent—have a change in our mind and become immersed in the flowing provisions of our Biblical salvation. The apostles are beseeching us to press on to receive the end of our faith and the saving of our souls which are in the hands of our benevolent resourceful heavenly Father.

Philippians 2:12-13 exhorts us to *"work out your own salvation with fear and trembling; for it is God who works in you both to will and to do for His good pleasure."* We have a sober and holy responsibility before God to cooperate with Him so that *"we may have confidence and not be ashamed before Him at His coming."* (1 Jn. 2:28) In this scenario the shame would be that we did not allow God to do in us what He purposefully and magnificently set out to do. I have discovered the following six matters of grace are our opportunity to co-labor with God in this salvation. For our part, we participate by receiving His grace, by letting grace do its work in us, by growing in grace, by being established in grace, by being strong in grace, and by standing in grace. Let us look at these six opportunities.

RECEIVING THE GRACE

John outlines the simple truth—*"As many as received Him to them He gave...."* (Jn. 1:12) This is what God does—He gives. We are the receivers. In the parable of the sower and the seed, what does the ground do but receive? What does the earth do but receive the rain from heaven? Do the lilies toil or are they clothed by God? Who feeds the birds of the air? We are so foolish! We strive and worry, fill our lives with anxiety about how we can possibly improve ourselves. We are sons of God! Our Father knows what we have need of and is resourceful enough to take care of His children. How much of our day are we preoccupied and misdirected by the one who comes to steal, kill, and destroy? We have been deceived into believing that only we can do what is required to improve our circumstances. Satan constantly is suggesting that God is too distant and disinterested. Nothing could be farther from the truth! We should learn from Bartimaeus. Do you recall the story?

> *"Now they came to Jericho. As He,* [Jesus] *went out of Jericho, with His disciples and a great multitude, blind Bartimaeus, the son of Timaeus, sat by the road begging. And when he heard that it was Jesus of Nazareth, he began to cry out and say, 'Jesus, Son of David, have mercy on me!' Then many warned him to be quiet; but he cried out all the more, 'Son of David, have mercy on me!' So Jesus stood still and commanded him to be called. Then they called the blind man, saying to him, 'Be of good cheer. Rise, He is calling you.' And throwing aside his garment, he rose and came to Jesus. So Jesus answered and said to him, 'What do you want Me to do for you?' The blind man said to Him, 'Rabboni, that I may receive my sight.' Then Jesus said to him, 'Go your way; your faith has made you well.' And immediately he received his sight and followed Jesus on the road."*

(Mark 10:46-52)

I love this story! Bartimaeus rises above the noise of the crowd, the obvious impossibility, and the critics who are trying to silence him. He shouts out to Jesus and shouts out again until he gets Jesus' attention. The only one that is interested in Bartimaeus is Jesus. How about that? Have you ever been in Bartimaeus' shoes? Have you experienced people ignoring you, putting you down, and trying to silence you? I am pretty sure you have. Cry out! Cry out to Jesus. He cares, and He is listening. *And*, Bartimaeus not only got a hearing before Jesus, he received his sight. One more not so small part of the story is that when Jesus told Bartimaeus to go his way, this man's choice was to follow Jesus. Things really change when we receive what Jesus is commissioned to distribute. This has got to be close to "living happily ever after." You want to give it a try?

Faith made Bartimaeus a receiver.

> *"So then faith comes by hearing, and hearing by the word of God."*
>
> (Rom. 10:17)

If the word of God is the source of faith, from whom does this *"word"* come? Who initiates it? Our heavenly Father sends it. It was the same with all the healings that Jesus did. No one earned healing from Jesus. Jesus was indebted to no one to heal them. Jesus is the Healer—the healed are the receivers. There is no effort on either side. The circle completed is giving and receiving.

Receiving seems like such a simple thing. Well, it is! At least it should be. Too often we complicate it with thoughts of worthiness and, of all things, suspicious reasonings of the motive of the giver. These kinds of suspicions should not occupy the heart of God's beloved children. As Father, God has ordained that *"All good giving* [lit. Greek] *and every perfect gift comes from above, and from the Father of the lights of heaven, with Him there is no variation, no play of passing shad-*

ows." (James 1:17 NEB) No resource can compare with Him. His resources are inexhaustible, and our Father is motivated by love that is eternal and man-centered. God's love is incomprehensible, for God is love. Since the Father's nature is such, we should have no difficulty with understanding that our Father wants to pour out the evidence of His love upon us. His greatest gift is His son Jesus. On this we can all agree.

I can almost see you nodding your head in agreement, and at the same time someone might be thinking, "This is so simplistic. Why make such a big deal of it in your book? Everyone knows that receiving is the way to be related to God." "Okay," I reply, "you are correct." However, since it is that simple, why are we not living a Christian life of total victory? Why are so many of the promises of God not evidently working in our daily living? Where is the power to heal, deliver, preach, set captives free, control our temper and tongue and personally live in the ascended victory of Jesus every minute of each day? The answer is that we are not yet very skillful in the matter of receiving. Nearly all of us are entangled with varying amounts of doubts, ignorance, and especially religious effort to earn "goodies" from God. Brothers and sisters, we should know by now that it doesn't work that way, but we seem to not know it. We self destruct with any number of combinations of the above. We stumble repeatedly because it is so simple. God knows how impotent we are. That is precisely why He made everything about our salvation as simple as receiving. Check your own success in the power and efficacy of God manifested in your daily life.

Is it possible that there is yet much we have to learn about this godly phenomenon of receiving from all the riches of His grace?

Now muse over this for a moment—how complicated was it to receive Jesus as Savior by faith? It is wonderfully easy! So it is with all the gifts from our heavenly Father. Jesus made the following remark to the religionists who were opposing Him.

> *"Ask, and it will be given to you; seek, and you will find; knock, and it will be opened to you. For everyone who asks receives, and he who seeks finds, and to him who knocks it will be opened. Or what man is there among you who, if his son asks for bread, will give him a stone? Or if he asks for a fish, will he give him a serpent? If you then, being evil, know how to give good gifts to your children, how much more will your Father who is in heaven give good things to those who ask Him!"*

(Matt. 7:7-11)

How obvious does the obvious have to be? Jesus was demonstrating the character of His Father. Paul puts it like this, *"And my God shall supply all your need according to His riches in glory by Christ Jesus. Now to our God and Father be glory forever and ever. Amen"* (Phil. 4:19-20). The overpowering focus here is not the matter of *"all your need,"* but rather *"according to His riches in glory."* He who cast the stars into space and gave all the flowers their hue has appointed Himself to be your caregiver. Why don't we let Him give to us everything that makes His heart happy?

Look at grace in action. In 2 Chronicles 16:9 we read, *"For the eyes of the Lord run to and fro throughout the whole earth, to show Himself strong in the behalf of them whose heart is perfect toward Him."* What does it mean to have a heart that is perfect toward Him? I submit to you that one who has learned to receive God's good giving is such a person. I think we all can safely agree that the person with a perfect heart toward God is not a sinless, perfect person. I am convinced that one who allows God to be *"I am that I am"* has a perfect heart toward God.

In the New Testament, John does not describe the physical birth of Jesus like Matthew and Luke do. John speaks only of the divine source of the man Jesus:

> *"In the beginning was the Word, and the Word was with God, and the Word was God. He was in the beginning with God. All things were made through Him, and without Him nothing was made that was made. He came to His own, and His own did not receive Him. But as many as received Him, to them He gave the right to become children of God, to those who believe in His name: …And the Word became flesh and dwelt among us, and we beheld His glory, the glory as of the only begotten of the Father, full of grace and truth. … And of His fullness we have all received, and grace for [Greek, "upon"] grace. For the law was given through Moses, but grace and truth came through Jesus Christ."*

(Jn. 1:1-3; 11-12,14,16-17)

In this passage, John reveals to us the law of grace: God gives—we receive. A person who has learned to receive God's grace reigns in His life. Paul tells us, *"For if by the one man's offense many died, much more the grace of God and the gift by the grace of the one Man, Jesus Christ, abounded to many...those who receive abundance of grace and of the gift of righteousness will reign in life through the one, Jesus Christ"* (Rom. 5:15,17). So, how much grace do you seem to need? God would say, "I have far more than that for you." According to Paul's words, we can surpass merely avoiding sin and the world. We can reign over all in Christ.

Death reigning in man was not optional or arbitrary; it was inescapable and final. Yet receiving grace is an optional matter, resulting from the exercise of the human will and faith in Jesus. Choosing to receive grace is fundamental and absolute. It is my choice to receive grace and reign in life. I say to myself and to all—receive!

LETTING GRACE DO ITS WORK

Let! Here is the key that opens every door to faith and victory in Jesus. This should not only intrigue and challenge us, but it should also be our way of life as Christians. When I get complicated in my mind about trying to live a good Christian life, I reduce things to this. Let Christ do what He uniquely does so well. Let Christ live the Christian life for me and in me. Jesus said, *"And He who sent Me is with Me. The Father has not left Me alone, for I always do those things that please Him"*

(Jn. 8:29). Jesus as a man lived the human and divine life in perfect harmony. It cannot be improved on by man or angels. So why don't we let God be involved in all our affairs? This may seem trite to the mind of the natural man. It is profound, however, because it is the good news—the gospel. Let God who delights to save us, save us. That just makes a lot of sense to me.

Here is a quick story as an example. On a trip driving from Houston to Dallas one afternoon, it began to mist a little. I was driving the speed limit when a van passed me traveling somewhat faster than that. As it went by, a small sensation clearly arose in my consciousness. Slow down. For whatever reason, I obeyed that intuitive suggestion. Within two minutes or so the driver of the van, now about a quarter of a mile in front of me, completely lost control of his vehicle. He did a 360, went off into the ditch and then back onto the highway in my lane, and then back and forth for a quarter of a mile. Had I not slowed down when I did, there would have been a terrible accident where we all may have been killed. I say again, God is determined to save us. We need to learn to let Him do that.

It is the same with every other spiritual encounter with God our Father. He has purposed to be a participant in all of our affairs. A major problem is that we are not allowing grace to labor as God purposes. Following are four passages that have been very helpful to me in the matter of letting the grace of God operate. They speak to me of who really needs to be in the driver's seat. There is something other than our natural inclination that should take over and lead us in living differently.

> *"Let this mind be in you which was also in Christ Jesus."*
>
> (Phil. 2:5)

> *"And let the peace of God rule in your hearts, to which also you were called in one body; and be thankful. Let the word of Christ dwell in you richly...."*
>
> (Col. 3:15-16)

> *"Therefore let that abide in you which you heard from the beginning. If what you heard from the beginning abides in you, you also will abide in the Son and in the Father. And this is the promise that He has promised us—eternal life."*
>
> (1 Jn. 2:24-25)

> *"But let patience have its perfect work, that you may be perfect and complete, lacking nothing. If any of you lacks wisdom, let him ask of God, who gives to all liberally and without reproach, and it will be given to him. But let him ask in faith, with no doubting, for he who doubts is like a wave of the sea driven and tossed by the wind."*
>
> (James 1:4-6)

"Let, let, let, let!" Now pause for a moment. Ruminate over these words from God. Do you see our inevitable involvement here? Your faith will grow and be enhanced remarkably if you will take heed to this matter seriously. Your understanding will be illuminated. The preceding verses present a state of being that seems heavenly. Guard them in your heart because Satan wants to steal this from you. Don't tolerate him doing that to you! Read the verses until praise and thanksgiving arise within your heart. Write them down. Memorize them. Quote them until they are irremovably etched in your brain. Allow God to do His good pleasure in you. This fundamentally means to turn to Christ in your spirit and allow Him to flow like a river of life into your soul. By such a flow, the streams of the authority and power of the Holy Spirit will begin to do the will of God in every aspect of your daily life. These streams of grace will refresh, empower, save, and guard you. And they shall perform all the will of God within you. "Let!" Now look at Colossians 1:3-7 again and consider what Paul told the Colossians how this was happening in them.

> *"We give thanks to God, the Father of our Lord Jesus Christ, praying always for you, since we heard of your faith in Christ Jesus and the love which you have for all the saints; because of the hope laid up for you in heaven, of which you previously heard in the word of truth, the gospel which has come to you, just as in all the world also it is constantly bearing fruit and increasing, even as it has been doing in you also since the day you heard of it and understood the grace of God in truth;"*

(NASB)

The word of the truth of the gospel had come to them, and it was bringing forth fruit and increasing. Fruitfulness is the natural outcome of the life which is flowing in the fruit tree. It is not a manufactured product. Do we really understand the operation of grace like these verses declare? We surely need to! Nature declares this truth all around us. The word of truth has come to each of us in the person of Christ. It is called the *"word of His grace"* (Acts 20:32). He is the seed of God's grace that is now bearing fruit and increasing within us. Our job is not obscure here. We must consistently let this happen according to the way that is designed and prescribed by God. Now that's not complicated, and that is precisely how we need to understand and experience the operation of the grace of God practically. If one starts to obsessively dig up the seed to assist its progress or even try to examine its development, great damage or at the least hindrance will occur. The Seed planted within our heart knows everything that is required for its growth, maturity, and fruitfulness. I need to be reminded again and again—let, let, let Him do the wondrous work of grace with its labor of love, and growth in the divine life. Our part is to water this seed through reading God's word, and prayer with thanksgiving.

To let is a proactive voluntary function of faith. It is just like opening your eyelid to allow the eye to see. God has provided the light for vision. He has made the eye with the functionality for vision. We just open the eyelid, and the eye spontaneously sees. Our part is simple and easy. We don't have to try to see, create the light or invent vision. That is all done by our Creator. We simply open the eyelid and seeing occurs. Do we have to command the eye to see? Does the earth struggle to absorb the rain? No! These are spontaneous events. It is no different in all our spiritual affairs—let!

Reconsider the familiar passage in Galatians 2:20-21.

> "I have been crucified with Christ; it is no longer I who live, but Christ lives in me; and the life which I now live in the flesh I live by faith in the Son of God, who loved me and gave Himself for me. I do not set aside the grace of God; for if righteousness comes through the law, then Christ died in vain."

The Bible clearly is informing us that Paul was a Christian that was living by someone else Who was supplying His faith for daily application. That is the power of grace. Paul's strong testimony declares that his manner of life was to receive the grace that was being supplied and to allow grace the opportunity to do God's will. Apply this to your every situation. Paul's part here was to let the grace function in him. The life is Christ's life and the faith is Christ's faith. For Paul to try to do something on his own would be setting the grace aside. The obvious conclusion is—that would not be the smart choice. What does it mean to set aside the grace of God? It is to ignore or reject what God has done and now freely gives to His children. God's fingerprints are all over this *letting* operation in Paul's living. This is crucially imperative for us to incorporate into our journey of faith. If we miss this step we are fallen from grace and into the captivity of trying to keep the law of Moses or whatever laws we have made up for ourselves. Remember that God said, *"this is My son in whom I am well pleased"* only to Jesus. There was no mention of John the Baptist or anyone else. Beloved saints, we cannot do anything better than Jesus. Let Him do it all through the Holy Spirit that dwells in you! What God our Father supremely enjoys is Christ in you! We should let Abba experience that joy all the time as we live every one of our days.

For many years I strived to work for God and serve Him. I had no idea that through most of that service I was setting aside grace and striving out of my own energy. Could this be the reason there is so much "burn out" among ministers and church leaders? When I read Paul's autobiographical sketch in 2 Corinthians, I am persuaded that he was a man who let grace operate in every kind of human situation. Here is some of that story:

> *"Blessed be the God and Father of our Lord Jesus Christ, the Father of mercies and God of all comfort, who comforts us in all our tribulation, that we may be able to comfort those who are in any trouble, with the comfort with which we ourselves are comforted by God. For as the sufferings of Christ abound in us, so our consolation also abounds through Christ. …For we do not want you to be ignorant, brethren, of our trouble which came to us in Asia: that we were burdened beyond measure, above strength, so that we despaired even of life. Yes, we had the sentence of death in ourselves, that we should not trust in ourselves but in God who*

raises the dead, who delivered us from so great a death, and does deliver us; in whom we trust that He will still deliver us, you also helping together in prayer for us, that thanks may be given by many persons on our behalf for the gift granted to us through many.

For our boasting is this: the testimony of our conscience that we conducted ourselves in the world in simplicity and godly sincerity, not with fleshly wisdom but by the grace of God, and more abundantly toward you.

(2 Cor. 1:3-5, 8-12)

Few Christians would volunteer for these trials. But here was a man who was under the operation of grace and living in the operation of grace. Some pretty serious stuff was going on in Paul's life. These things sound like overwhelming circumstances. But Paul had learned to look to God who was in control of everything that seemed out of control.

I can't resist sharing my experience in this matter of knowing God as my comforter. He does not come to me in times of testing as One patting my head, holding my hand and saying, "There, there—everything is going to be alright. Are you ok?" Not so! I'm not kidding. Mostly I experience the comfort of God as a dynamic interruption of Abba who says, "Hey Herman, I know this is tough. My Son went through this stuff too. I was with Him through every step of the way, and I am here with you just the same as then. I'm here son; I've got this matter in hand, and I've got you covered. Don't worry or go negative on Me. I not only understand the present situation, I know what's ahead. Keep leaning on Me! My plan is working great, and you're securely in My hands. Got it? Now here we go—on one!"

When Paul was praying for deliverance from the thorn in his flesh, the Heavenly Father graciously came to remind Paul to stay in the operation of grace. That grace was surpassing the need by far and was perfect in the situation. I have heard it said many times, "Let go, and let God…!" This is definitely what we need to learn today.

> *"Now may the God of hope fill you with all joy and peace in believing, that you may abound in hope by the power of the Holy Spirit."*
>
> (Rom. 15:13)

Did you notice that it is by the power of the Holy Spirit? Saints, let God do His work in you and all His other children. He can do it!

Having stated these things about letting grace operate in us, I emphatically must declare that *"to let"* is not to be passive. Jesus was not passive. The apostles were not passive. They were laying hold of the grace that was being supplied by God. The command to *"draw near to God"* shatters the notion of passivity. To *"resist the devil"* is not passive. We are charged to be very proactive in this matter. Consider the "great commission" of Jesus in Matthew 28:18-20. All authority in heaven and on earth is given to Jesus. He says, *"Therefore."* That means "because of this" *you* go; *you* make disciples; *you* teach; *you* baptize. Then Jesus concludes by saying the key to everything. He says, *"Lo, I am with you."* When we receive revelation of this vital point, everything will change in our life with Christ. We will still come boldly to the throne of grace, but Christ will be doing the work in us and through us! Let Him do it. He is great at what He does. Hallelujah!

GROWING IN GRACE

Having learned to receive grace and allow grace to operate freely in us, now we can go on to experience the dynamics of growing in grace. Grow is a common word to us all. What it implies is wonderful. I hope that our familiarity with the word will not obscure our appreciation of the reality of how it is life in a changing mode. Everything that is organic is changing. The spiritual implication for us should fill our hearts with unspeakable joy! Our destiny as Christians is to change through growth as is pointed out in the following verses.

> *"So why do you worry about clothing? Consider the lilies of the field, how they grow: they neither toil nor spin; and yet I say to you that even Solomon in all his glory was not arrayed like one of these. Now if God so clothes the grass of the field, which today is, and tomorrow is thrown into the oven, will He not much more clothe you, O you of little faith?"*
>
> (Matt. 6:28-30)

> *"And He* [Jesus] *said, 'The kingdom of God is as if a man should scatter seed on the ground, and should sleep by night and rise by day, and the seed should*

sprout and grow, he himself does not know how. For the earth yields crops by itself: first the blade, then the head, after that the full grain in the head. But when the grain ripens, immediately he puts in the sickle, because the harvest has come.'"

(Mark 4:26-29)

"As newborn babes, desire the pure milk of the word, [in order] *that you may grow thereby, if indeed you have tasted that the Lord is gracious."*

(1 Pet. 2:2-3)

"I planted, Apollos watered, but God was causing the growth."

(1 Cor. 3:6 NASB)

I hope that you thoroughly appreciate the powerful impact of this last verse. "God causes the growth." Please, let the Holy Spirit form and guide your thinking about how you grow up into Christ. Can you add to your stature? God makes to grow! The need for growth in the Christian life is understood by nearly all believers. As it is with the human body, so it is with our spiritual life in Christ. Do we understand, however, that the factor of our growth is through God's grace? 2 Peter 3:18 tells us, *"…but grow in the grace and knowledge of our Lord and Savior Jesus Christ."* What is this grace in which we are to grow? It is everything about God that is to be apprehended by us. In 1 Peter 3:7 we are told, *"Husbands, likewise, dwell with them* [your wife] *with understanding, giving honor to the wife, as to the weaker vessel, and as being heirs together of the grace of life."* Now there is a practical example. Let grace be your essence in your relationship with your wife—kids, grandkids, and in-laws. Implied here but often overlooked is the matter of grace operating in the life growing process. To live with our wives or husbands is a down-to-earth matter. Need I say that sometimes it is a strain? The effective way to live in peace together is to do it by growing in grace together. To date, everything else that I have tried crashed and burned. I say to myself, "Herman, keep your eye on the ball. Grow in grace!"

The phrase "grace of life" is an extraordinary phrase. It appears only once in the New Testament. The word translated "life" in this phrase is the Greek word "zoe." Zoe is almost exclusively used in the New Testament to speak of the divine life—God's life. Its implication is exceedingly profound. The complete divine person of the triune God is in this grace of life. Since Christ is the embodiment of the Godhead, this *"grace of life"* is Christ Himself in His victorious, transcendent state! The grace in "zoe" life is always in motion. It is the energy of life moving economically within every Christian soul. As we "let" this life move in us, we spontaneously grow. Amazing! That is why it is called the anointing in 2 John 2:20 and 27.

> *"But you have an anointing from the Holy one, and you know all things. ...But the anointing which you have received from Him abides in you, and you do not need that anyone teach you; but as the same anointing teaches you concerning all things, and is true, and is*

not a lie, and just as it has taught you, you will
abide in Him."

It is the kinetic power of our resurrected Jesus charging our batteries all the time. The reason I refer to this verse is because we need to notice that the word "anointing" is a verbal noun. There is action going on here, and that action results in growth. The bar is set pretty high. Does your spouse live with someone who emanates the grace of life? Well, don't get condemned about it. Keep growing in life. Receive (as in seize) today's portion of grace; let it operate unhindered in you; watch yourself grow up into Christ in all things.

Paul tells us in Philippians 1:7, *"You all are partakers with me of grace."* Grace is for every believer regardless of the appearance of their current condition. It is in Christ as grace to us all that the children of God are able to grow. God loves and honors all of us with equality and will not withhold His grace from anyone. This grace is the supplied access and availability of everything that God is and has done in Christ for our deliverance and salvation. That means that Christ is the sphere in whom we *"live and move and have our being."* Acts 17:27-28 tells us, *"...He is not far from each one of us; for in Him we live and move and have our being...."*

This is the *"bountiful supply of the Spirit of Jesus Christ"* (Phil. 1:19). This Christ of supply is within our human spirit. He totally occupies our whole spirit. Therefore to have such a life within us that is moving from our spirit into our soul is the function of growing in the grace of life. That is what Paul pointed out in Colossians chapter 1.

"…Giving thanks to the Father who has qualified us to be partakers of the inheritance of the saints in the light. He has delivered us from the power of darkness and conveyed us into the kingdom of the Son of His love, in whom we have redemption through His blood, the forgiveness of sins. He is the image of the invisible God, the firstborn over all creation. For by Him all things were created that are in heaven and that are on earth, visible and invisible, whether thrones or dominions or principalities or powers. All things were created through Him and for Him. And He is before all things, and in Him all things consist. And He is the head of the body, the church, Who is the beginning, the firstborn from the dead, that in all things He may have the preeminence."

(Col. 1:12-18)

Paul is saying that our saving Jesus is supreme over everything. Jesus holds everything together—including you and me—and He is the governor of everything in heaven and on earth. The awesome Christ that is identified in these verses is now overseeing our daily growth. Since Christ is so preeminent, and He is in us, it is difficult not to grow. A Christian has to intentionally ignore and neglect this wonderful Christ to not grow up in Him. And as described in the preceding verses, there is a magnificent and awesome Christ to grow into. To be stubborn and to refuse to grow up into our preeminent Jesus requires a lot of diabolical help. From whence comes your help? You and I get to make the choice.

Paul continues this theme of growing in Colossians 2:19. *"...holding fast to the Head, from whom all the body, nourished and knit together by joints and ligaments, grows with the increase that is from God."* And again in Ephesians 2:19-22 Paul explains,

> *"Now, therefore, you are no longer strangers and foreigners, but fellow citizens with the saints and members of the household of God, having been built on the foundation of the apostles and prophets, Jesus Christ Himself being the chief cornerstone, in whom the whole building, being fitted together, grows into a holy temple in the Lord, in whom you also are being built together for a dwelling place of God in the Spirit."*

To grow into a holy temple of the Lord is to become God's eternal habitation. Each one of us is particularly placed in the body of Christ in order that there would be no lack in the manifestation of the *"glory of His grace."* (Eph. 1:6) No one can replace you—each one of us is indispensable. You must grow. I must grow. We grow in grace. Paul went on to admonish us in Ephesians 4:15 that we may *"grow up in all things into Him who is the head."* I believe that the growth that each one of us experiences is recognized in the celestial realm as a portion of God's glory manifested on earth in mankind. This is called the glory of His grace. We may not be aware of what is happening in us as being glorious, but I am reluctant to argue with the biblical language. What goes on in us each time we experience the riches of God's grace must make the angels gasp with awe.

Think of it. You and I have the opportunity to grow up into the Christ described in Colossians 1:12-18. And we may grow up into Him in every situation that confronts us. Why don't we seize every occasion in our living to grow up into Christ with this kind of heavenly vision? The more we grow, the more we are enriched by Christ. That is His commission and He will get it done.

> *"Grace to you and peace from God our Father and the Lord Jesus Christ. I thank my God always concerning you for the grace of God which was given to you by Christ Jesus, that you were enriched in everything by Him in all utterance and all knowledge, even as the testimony of Christ was confirmed in you, so that you come short in no gift, eagerly waiting for the revelation of our Lord Jesus Christ, who will also confirm you to the end, that you may be blameless in the day of our Lord Jesus Christ. God is faithful, by whom you were called into the fellowship of His Son, Jesus Christ our Lord."*

(1 Cor. 1:3-9)

This is the testimony of Paul encouraging the saints in the church in Corinth. These saints, who had experienced abounding grace from God, still had significant problems. They needed to continue growing in grace. Although Paul's commendation of them at the beginning of his letter is so marvelous, the following chapters clearly indicate that the believers in Corinth had a lot of growing to do. They were folks just like us. For them and us the journey is one of growing up into Christ Jesus in everything. We must continue to be "enriched in everything by Him." This is a constant life-long work of grace. Our growing and being enriched by grace will overcome all Christlessness that troubles us now. Please, do not compare yourself with any other Christian and get discouraged. Even the best Christian that you know or have ever met still has room and needs to grow if he is still alive. The more clearly we see this vision of growing in grace, the more confidently we will be established in the truth and in our faith. We will come to the throne of grace with more joy and boldness.

BEING ESTABLISHED IN GRACE

Now we come to the matter of being established in the grace that is being supplied without interruption from God our Father. Peter encourages the believers in this way.

> *"But may the God of all grace, who called us to His eternal glory by Christ Jesus, after you have suffered a while, perfect, establish, strengthen, and settle you."*

(1 Pet. 5:10)

How about this description of God—the God of all grace? By so much grace He called us to His eternal glory. On the way the God of all grace is perfecting, establishing, strengthening and settling each of us.

I feel secure in what Abba is doing. God is always occupied with lavishing the riches of His grace upon us. It is His preoccupying desire that we be established in as much of His grace as we can absorb. The more we grow, the more we are confident in our relationship with God. We look at things that surround us differently. We are not so easily discouraged. We find that there is boldness in our soul when beset by the evil strategies of the devil. We are being established in the faith. Because of this, Paul prays to the Father, "... *that you may be filled with all the fullness of God*" (Eph. 3:19). The measure of the grace given to each one of us is to transfer to us the effective operation of God. His ministry effectively flowed through Christ. Now the same mission and ministry are to flow through all the members of the body of Christ. Therefore we need to be established in the grace of God. Consider Paul's statement in Romans 1:11-12. *"For I long to see you, that I may impart to you some spiritual gift, so that you may be established—that is, that I may be encouraged together with you by the mutual faith both of you and me."*

Paul longed for all the saints to participate fully in the abundant supply of grace. He knew that they and he needed to be able to grow in God's grace in order to withstand the efforts of Satan to overrun their confidence in Jesus as Savior and the effectiveness of that saving work to be effective in all who believe. He knew that he had experienced a lot of grace. And he knew that other believers had also. He was not so occupied with his portion that he didn't need grace that was constantly being deposited in others. Listen again to his words in Colossians 1:9-11.

> *"For this reason we also, since the day we heard it, do not cease to pray for you, and to ask that you*

*may be filled with the knowledge of His will in all
wisdom and spiritual understanding; that you may
walk worthy of the Lord, fully pleasing Him, being
fruitful in every good work and increasing in the
knowledge of God; strengthened with all might,
according to His glorious power, for all patience
and longsuffering with joy."*

Verses like these are so compact with superlative
language that faith responds with resounding worship.
As this prayer is fulfilled in all the believers, many practical evidences of grace will be manifested in their lives.
This is what happens when we are being established in
the grace of God. In the formative days of the spreading
of the faith from Jerusalem to Antioch, Barnabas was
sent to Antioch to find out what had happened there.

*"Then news of these things came to the ears of the
church in Jerusalem, and they sent out Barnabas to
go as far as Antioch. When he came and had seen
the grace of God, he was glad, and encouraged them
all that with purpose of heart they should continue
with the Lord. For he was a good man, full of the
Holy Spirit and of faith. And a great many people
were added to the Lord."*

(Acts 11:22-24)

Whatever grace had done among the believers was
visible. *"And with great power the apostles gave witness to
the resurrection of the Lord Jesus. And great grace was upon
them all"* (Acts 4:33). Beloved, that is routine when
the Holy Spirit is establishing people in grace. Those
who had received this grace preached Him whom they

believed; they believed Him whom they preached; and they did signs and wonders through His name. The signs and wonders were very visible. From the moment of their believing, the Holy Spirit began to establish these believers in the grace of God. The more they grew in the knowledge of God, the more they were established in their faith. In this faith they were allowing the Holy Spirit to do miraculous things. Nothing has changed from God's perspective. Let us believe and preach boldly in Jesus' name. God's works of power will again be manifested in your life and mine. In this process of growth we too will be established in faith and grace. The result will be as visible in us as it was in the early church. Our faith will be like an oak tree whose roots are going down deeply into the ground with each year's growth. With that establishing growth the oak can withstand nature's storms. This is what the early Christians were experiencing through the ministry of the apostles. Being established like this is God's will for us in our church and community.

> *"Now it happened in Iconium that they* [Paul and Barnabas] *went together to the synagogue of the Jews, and so spoke that a great multitude both of the Jews and of the Greeks believed.... Therefore they stayed there a long time, speaking boldly in the Lord, who was bearing witness to the word of His grace, granting signs and wonders to be done by their hands."*
>
> (Acts 14:1-3)

What Paul referred to in Colossians 2:6-7 had happened to these believers. *"As you therefore have received Christ Jesus the Lord, so walk in Him, rooted and built up in Him and established in the faith, as you have been taught, abounding in it with thanksgiving."* The believers had received Christ by faith and now they were being established through faith in the same manner. We pointed out before, that the brothers and sisters had begun to minister out of the measure of the gift of Christ's grace. That is exactly what Paul had admonished the Roman believers to do.

> *"Having then gifts differing according to the grace that is given to us, let us use them: if prophecy, let us prophesy in proportion to our faith; or ministry, let us use it in our ministering; he who teaches, in teaching; he who exhorts, in exhortation; he who gives, with liberality; he who leads, with diligence; he who shows mercy, with cheerfulness."*
>
> (Rom. 12:6-8)

All our functioning in daily life, family, on the job, and in the church should be done *"according to the grace given to us."* Being occupied in the labor of God has a lot to do with what establishes us in grace. Our confidence in His ability and reliability is steadily reinforced. When we see God perform His works through us and others, we are firmly established in faith. Our roots sink deeper into the wonders of His grace. We know that we know Him. The key to such a firm assurance of His reliability is in our co-laboring with Him. We see the

Jesus Christ of the Bible doing acts of power in our time, in our town, in our family, in our life. Our experience with Him becomes our confidence to labor more with faith in His grace. I am learning to thank the Lord each day for grace. This is transforming my perception. Now I live my days in expectation of something wonderful happening.

I remember driving home one day from visiting a friend, and Jesus spoke into my heart. He said, "Herman, begin to expect the unexpected." Some rather remarkable things have happened to me since that time. Is there a similar expectation stirring in your soul as you start your day? If there are days that are not like this, lay hold of more grace that is awaiting you. I assure you that you will not be disappointed with His supply. This relentless pursuit in faith that grace is already on its way is a real confidence builder. Paul himself practiced this way. He planted. Others watered, and God made to grow. When you see the sprout of the seeds you have planted, assurance is yours. God did that, and you had a part in it!

> "For we are God's fellow workers; you are God's field, you are God's building. According to the grace of God which was given to me, as a wise master builder I have laid the foundation, and another builds on it. But let each one take heed how he builds on it. For no other foundation can anyone lay than that which is laid, which is Jesus Christ."
>
> (1 Cor. 3:9-11)

Jesus Himself served in this way.

> *"For you know the grace of our Lord Jesus Christ, that though He was rich, yet for your sakes He became poor, that you through His poverty might become rich."*

(2 Cor. 8:9)

There was great expectation in everything Jesus did because He was relying on God to do what was needed. By grace Jesus was enabled to leave everything He had in heaven to come as a poor man to help us become rich. He did it all for our benefit; this is why we are rich in His grace. By growing in the riches of his grace, we are established in grace to serve others in the same way. The more we are established in grace, the greater will be our effectiveness in co-laboring with God and enriching others.

In Romans 12:8, Paul speaks of those who give. They do it with liberality. In 2 Corinthians 9, he continues this theme of liberality existing and operating in the saints.

> *"But this I say: He who sows sparingly will also reap sparingly, and he who sows bountifully will also reap bountifully. So let each one give as he purposes in his heart, not grudgingly or of necessity; for God loves a cheerful giver. And God is able to make all grace abound toward you, that you, always having all sufficiency in all things, may have an abundance for every good work. As it is written:*
> *'He has dispersed abroad,*
> *He has given to the poor;*

His righteousness endures forever.'
Now may He who supplies seed to the sower,
and bread for food, supply and multiply the seed
you have sown and increase the fruits of your right-
eousness, while you are enriched in everything for
all liberality, which causes thanksgiving through us
to God."

(2 Cor. 9:6-10)

I do not submit these verses as they are most frequently used in order to raise money. My purpose in
using them is to point out that these saints were firmly
established in the power of grace. Of course anything
that touches our money touches deep seated issues in
our hearts. These saints were going beyond their ability
to care for others whom they probably had never seen.
It is grace that makes this possible. Paul points out
in verse seven that God loves a "cheerful" [lit. hilari-
ous] giver. How can any person give away their money
with hilarity? Grace was working mightily. When you
read this section of the Word, observe the superlative
phrases in the language. The Spirit of grace had profoundly enriched the believers with God's nature of
love of sharing.

God was teaching and establishing them in the labor
of grace. Notice how much was going on between God
and the believers. God and His family were all caught
up in giving to each other. Notice too what effect it had
on the things that were happening among the saints.
They were being well established in the liberality of
the divine nature. God as provider is transmitting His
nature of giving lavishly, hilariously, into His dear chil-

dren. Not only were the saints generous, they loved and prayed for their brothers in the churches. And this was called the "exceeding grace" that was in them. This is powerful evidence of what being established in grace is all about.

> *"While through the proof of this ministry, they glo-*
> *rify God for the obedience of your confession to the*
> *gospel of Christ, and for your liberal sharing with*
> *them and all men, and by their prayer for you, who*
> *long for you because of the exceeding grace of God*
> *in you. Thanks be to God for His indescribable gift!"*

(2 Cor. 9:13-15)

In the previous chapter, Paul spoke of the liberality of the brethren in Macedonia, describing them in this way:

> *"Moreover, brethren, we make known to you the*
> *grace of God bestowed on the churches of Macedonia:*
> *that in a great trial of affliction the abundance of*
> *their joy and their deep poverty abounded in the*
> *riches of their liberality. For I bear witness that*
> *according to their ability, yes, and beyond their*
> *ability, they were freely willing, imploring us*
> *with much urgency that we would receive the gift*
> *and the fellowship of the ministering to the saints.*
> *And not only as we had hoped, but they first gave*
> *themselves to the Lord, and then to us by the will*
> *of God."*

(2 Cor. 8:1-5)

To my estimation, these people were quite established in the character of God. Though these passages are referring to sharing with others in material and financial ways, the principal of giving in God's giving applies to every area of our Christian experience. God inspires a desire in your heart to do something or obey His prompting. You respond in faith and action. God renders a planned result. You see it and rejoice. Your faith and confidence in Him grows because you followed the prompt of the Spirit and saw that God was doing something. Somehow you know that you have done something with God, and God has done something with you. You are established in His grace, and you know it. There is no doubt in you that He initiated the action and produced the end result.

A brother through whom God was ministering healing recently told me, "Herman, there is nothing like seeing God heal someone through you." Isn't the same true of anything that God does through His people? It firmly establishes us in His grace. This surely includes the smallest of functions of any action of God through the least of all saints.

Furthermore, grace establishes the saints in the way they speak to one another. This matter of words spoken is a profound issue of grace in the New Testament. Jesus said. *"The words that I speak to you are spirit, and they are life."* (Jn. 6:63) What Jesus spoke ministered life to people because He was *"full of grace and truth."* When Jesus began His ministry, even His reading of the scripture supplied grace to those who were hearing Him.

> *"So He* [Jesus] *came to Nazareth, where He had been brought up. And as His custom was, He went*

into the synagogue on the Sabbath day, and stood up to read. And He was handed the book of the prophet Isaiah. And when He had opened the book, He found the place where it was written:

'The Spirit of the LORD *is upon Me,*
Because he has anointed Me
To preach the gospel to the poor;
He has sent Me to heal the brokenhearted,
To proclaim liberty to the captives
And recovery of sight to the blind,
To set at liberty those who are oppressed;
To proclaim the acceptable year of the LORD.*'*

Then he closed the book, and gave it back to the attendant and sat down. And the eyes of all who were in the synagogue were fixed on Him. And He began to say to them, 'Today this Scripture is fulfilled in your hearing.' So all bore witness to Him, and marveled at the gracious words which proceeded out of His mouth."

(Luke 4:16-22)

In the early experience of those in the churches, speaking through and with grace was common. It is the same with us who have received Christ. As we are growing in grace, our words spoken will convey grace to others. We are being established in grace; we are learning to speak out of the grace that is within us. This speaking is anointed with the substance of the Lord Jesus Himself; thus, it has a tremendous impact on the people who hear us. Sometimes when a brother or sisters is responding to challenging attacks of unbelievers, I marvel at the wisdom in their answers. God was obviously supplying those words. I used to think that those folks were just clever people. Not so now. Now I realize that they are saints who have a working measure of grace which has firmly established them in Christ Jesus. They have learned to let grace operate in their thinking and speaking.

On the positive side, Paul admonished the Colossians, *"Let your speech always be with grace, seasoned with salt, that you may know how you ought to answer each one"* (Col. 4:6). On the corrective side, Paul said this to the brethren,

> *"Let no corrupt word proceed out of your mouth, but what is good for necessary edification, that it may impart grace to the hearers. And do not grieve the Holy Spirit of God, by whom you were sealed for the day of redemption."*

(Eph. 4:29-30)

The common experience of the believers was to be one of speaking out of the abundance of grace which they were themselves enjoying. Since this was their habit, then those who heard them were impacted by God Himself. To fail to speak with words seasoned with grace would be a grief to the Holy Spirit. We too are endowed with grace to speak gracious words.

> *"Therefore do not be unwise, but understand what the will of the Lord is. But be filled with the Spirit, speaking to one another in psalms and hymns and spiritual songs, singing and making melody in your heart to the Lord, giving thanks always for all*

172

things to God the Father in the name of our Lord Jesus Christ."

(Eph. 5:17-20)

Gracious words were coming from the infilling of the Spirit. These words of grace were transported in their speaking to each other, in their singing of hymns, and in their meetings. As a result their hearts were full of melody and they were able to give thanks to God for all things. Consider how Paul spoke to the Roman believers out of grace.

"For I say, through the grace given to me, to every-one who is among you, not to think of himself more highly than he ought to think, but to think soberly, as God has dealt to each one a measure of faith."

(Rom. 12:3)

When I read this verse, I admire the ease with which Paul speaks about such a significant matter as exhorting the church not to be proud. When you try to help someone who is absorbed with himself, it is paramount that you be full of grace. Paul had learned how to minister grace to his hearers. Those of us who have a rather large ego know that we need to let the Lord deal with our speaking. Yet our chatter seems to linger. But the main point here is how Paul approaches this and places it in this magnificent chapter on the body of Christ. *"I say through the grace…."* I worship God for this. What grace did in Paul's soul, grace will do in you and me. Isn't that just what you would expect God to do? Well,

He is committed to do it. Amen! Praise the Lord we are learning to let grace do its work in us. The more we utilize each moment's grace, the more we shall be established in Christ. There is still much saving grace to explore, discover, and dispense as the gospel.

BEING STRONG IN GRACE

The next area of grace we need to enter into is the strength that being established in grace provides. We believers must be strong in grace to do the work of the gospel for the advancement of the kingdom of God. I encourage you to meditate on the following verses:

> *"Finally, my brethren, be strong in the Lord and in the power of His might."*

(Eph. 6:10)

> *"You therefore, my son, be strong in the grace that is in Christ Jesus."*

(2 Tim. 2:1)

> *"I have written to you, young men, because you are strong, and the word of God abides in you, and you have overcome the wicked one."*

(1 Jn. 2:14)

Strengthening is a matter of being exercised in any matter. We all understand being strong in the physical realm. Paul told Timothy,

"If you instruct the brethren in these things, you will be a good minister of Jesus Christ, nourished in the words of faith and of the good doctrine which you have carefully followed. But reject profane and old wives' fables, and exercise yourself toward godliness. For bodily exercise profits a little, but godliness is profitable for all things, having promise of the life that now is and of that which is to come."

(1 Tim. 4:6-8)

I suppose that a large percentage of Christians aspire to be strong and overcome things like sin, the world, addictions, weakness, and a plethora of other things. If you asked 100 Christians if they considered themselves to be strong disciples of Christ, perhaps very few of them would answer yes. I doubt that the reason is a matter of humility. It must be said, however, that a growing number of believers are learning to live in the victory of Christ in a consistent way. I believe the key to discovering why is in the verses quoted at the start of the section.

Paul uses two very significant words in the passage to Timothy quoted above that need our attention. First observe the word *"nourished."* This is a matter of internalizing something as when we eat food. The food we eat becomes the very nourishment that our body requires. In this case Paul was admonishing Timothy to take in the scriptures by reading them faithfully. The second word comes out of the first. It is *"minister."* Here to minister means to serve others as a waiter serves food to someone. We ourselves must receive nourishment from the divine word of God. In fellowship with Him over His word we will be empowered by the Person of the Word. It is from this personal empowerment that we are enabled to serve to others the essence of Jesus Christ Who has become our life. This kind of ministry is prevailing.

Isn't it amazing that God not only secured our redemption but also wants us to prevail over all Satan's temptations and attempts to trouble us? To accomplish this, God has chosen the way of nourishing us through faith and grace. While we read and meditate on the Word of God, we are nourished by it. This nourishment becomes our inward constitution—the strength of our inner man. By this process of nourishment, we become obedient to the reality of what the Holy Spirit speaks to us. Of course our obedience should always correspond with the Bible as the Word of God. The harmony between what the Spirit leads us to do and the Bible's teaching is perfect. Do you expect to be strong in the Lord? If the answer is yes, then I would ask, "How much time do you spend in intimate fellowship with the Lord over His Word? Remember that we Christians are people of faith. And faith comes by hearing and hearing by the Word of God. Our strength is directly related to what and how much we eat.

Let's take the following scripture for a little test. In Philippians 4:13 Paul proclaims, *"I can do all things through Christ who strengthens me."* You have heard this quoted from pastors, your friends, and you have probably said it yourself. The question that arises in my mind when people quote this passage is, "Where are they putting their emphasis?"

Some years ago when I was considering this verse, I began to wonder about this for myself. I read the verse several times, emphasizing a different word each time. I realized that I had always put my emphasis on *"I can."* I asked the Lord to show me what He wanted me to understand about this statement. Soon it became apparent to me that the proper emphasis should be on the word *"through."* Look at the literal translation of the verse: *"All things I am strong for in the empowering me Christ."* What a huge difference dawned in my understanding. A verse that helped me in coming to this conclusion was Colossians 3:17. It admonishes us in this way, *"And whatever you do in word or deed, do all in the name of the Lord Jesus,* [in His person] *giving thanks to God the Father through Him."* Do you see what I mean? Whatever we do, we do it *"through"* Jesus as the agent and the reality. This is an example of how musing in the word, with the Spirit of grace guiding us, can bring revelation and strength to do the will of God (by letting Him do it in us). Why don't you give this a try yourself and see what happens?

Since Christ is our life, He should be our living. If I go to work, I should go to work with Jesus as my reality (the substance of my person). In speaking to someone, that someone should be hearing the voice of the Lord. I suppose that thousands of sincere Christians have been taken captive with the thought, "What would Jesus do?" For most, I think that this is a mental exercise of trying to do no more than to arrive at the "right" thing to do. That is, what would Jesus probably do? I've discovered that Jesus did not do this—ever. He did what the Father was doing every time. He never tried to imitate God the Father. He lived by the Father. His living, speaking, and working were the life, words, and labor of the Father through Him. Jesus said:

> "*When you lift up the Son of Man, then you will know that I am He, and that I do nothing of Myself; but as My Father taught Me, I speak these things. And He who sent Me is with Me. The Father has not left Me alone, for I always do those things that please Him.*"

(Jn. 8:28-29)

This was the strength and authority indwelling the person of our Lord. As Jesus and the Father are one, so also we are one with the Father in Jesus. To be strong in the Lord, therefore, is to be consistent in allowing Him to live out His life through us. We are firmly attached to Jesus, and Jesus becomes the *"doer"* in us.

Again I refer to Colossians 1:9-12 as an excellent example of what we are talking about.

> "*For this reason we also, since the day we heard it, do not cease to pray for you, and to ask that you may be filled with the knowledge of His will in all wisdom and spiritual understanding; that you may walk worthy of the Lord, fully pleasing Him, being fruitful in every good work and increasing in the knowledge of God; strengthened with all might, according to His glorious power, for all patience*

and longsuffering with joy; giving thanks to the Father who has qualified us to be partakers of the inheritance of the saints in the light."

Such human living proceeds from the operation of the law of the Spirit of Life within us. We are strengthened according to His glorious power, not by our useless effort to be like Him. Apart from Christ everything else is still under the power of darkness, regardless of how good it may appear. If we are not living in the reality of Christ living through us, we are not experiencing deliverance from the power of darkness. Our strength issues from Him alone. This is what living in the new creation is like! Be strengthened in Paul's affirmation: *"Finally, my brethren, be strong in the Lord and in the power of His might."* (Eph. 6:10) As Jesus was strong through living by His Father, we also obtain our strength through living by Christ.

Recall Paul's autobiographical words:

"But by the grace of God I am what I am, and His grace toward me was not in vain; but I labored more abundantly than they all, yet not I, but the grace of God which was with me."

(1 Cor. 15:10)

Paul was a murderer and persecutor of the believers in Christ. What an evil man! But the grace of God came to rescue him. Grace rescued Paul not from being an evil man to being a good man. No! Grace liberated Paul to live in and by the life of God in Christ. It can be and should be the same in our living. We are liberated and made strong by another life coming to live in us and become the life we now live. That life is Jesus, and He is strong! Paul was so strong in the faith that he could rebuke Peter to his face before the assembled church when Peter failed to walk in truth and the impartial love of Christ

Think about Paul's experience with Barnabas for a moment. They got into a big argument about taking Mark with them on their second mission trip to the Gentile churches. They parted company and probably had some strong feelings of frustration and resentment. Mark had abandoned Paul and Barnabas on the first missionary trip, and Paul did not feel that Mark was qualified to go with them again on the upcoming trip. However, the Spirit of grace worked in Paul's heart regarding Mark. We have a window of this in the letter to the saints in Colossae.

> "Aristarchus my fellow prisoner greets you, with Mark the cousin of Barnabas (about whom you received instructions: if he comes to you, welcome him)."

(Col. 4:10)

Paul was so strong in the grace that he could truthfully say:

> "For you yourselves know how you ought to follow us, for we were not disorderly among you; nor did we eat anyone's bread free of charge, but worked with labor and toil night and day, that we might not be a burden to any of you, not because we do not

have authority, but to make ourselves an example
of how you should follow us."

(2 Thess. 3:7-9)

Paul had the strength of character to provide for his own physical and personal needs as well as the needs of those traveling with him. Of course others should have taken care of this minister of the gospel, but Paul had rather take care of himself than be indebted to others who might think that he had taken advantage of them. He loved his converts as Jesus loved us. He emptied himself of his rights in order for others to benefit. This is how Paul demonstrated what being strong in the Lord means. He was allowing the resources and presence of Jesus in his own life to become the strength through which he ministered to others.

Paul recommended Epaphroditus as a strong believer who served the interest of the saints well.

"Yet I considered it necessary to send to you
Epaphroditus, my brother, fellow worker, and fel-
low soldier, but your messenger and the one who
ministered to my need; since he was longing for you
all, and was distressed because you had heard that
he was sick. For indeed he was sick almost unto
death; but God had mercy on him, and not only
on him but on me also, lest I should have sorrow
upon sorrow. Therefore I sent him the more eagerly,
that when you see him again you may rejoice, and
I may be less sorrowful. Receive him therefore in
the Lord with all gladness, and hold such men in
esteem; because for the work of Christ he came close

> to death, not regarding his life, to supply what was
> lacking in your service toward me."

(Phil. 2:25-30)

Timothy served Paul and the churches in a similar manner of strength:

> "You therefore, my son, be strong in the grace that is
> in Christ Jesus. And the things that you have heard
> from me among many witnesses, commit these to
> faithful men who will be able to teach others also.
> You therefore must endure hardship as a good sol-
> dier of Jesus Christ. No one engaged in warfare
> entangles himself with the affairs of this life, that
> he may please him who enlisted him as a soldier."

(2 Tim. 2:1-4)

Christ manifested the strength and power of God because He was living in the presence of His Father. We can live by Christ who now is our life in the same way. He is our strength for all daily affairs.

Now let's review this matter about being strong in the Lord. We get our strength from what we eat and how we exercise. Our nourishment is the words that proceed from God. We must spend our time with the Word as it is our necessary food. Indeed it is! Without the ingested Word we will languish and be unprofitable servants of the Lord. Herein is the exercise. Develop a manner of life that sets aside time to read and pon-der what the Bible presents. It is a discipline without which we will be faint before our enemies and circum-stances. Remember Jesus said, *"The words that I speak to you are spirit, and they are life"* (John 6:63). The life and strength of God are in His words. To read, meditate, pray, and speak the words of the Bible is our exercise in the spirit that is profitable unto godliness.

STANDING IN GRACE

> *"Be sober; be vigilant; because your adversary the devil walks about like a roaring lion, seeking whom he may devour. Resist him, steadfast in the faith, knowing that the same sufferings are experienced by your brotherhood in the world. But may the God of all grace, who called us to His eternal glory by Christ Jesus, after you have suffered a while, perfect, establish, strengthen, and settle you. To Him be the glory and the dominion forever and ever. Amen."*

(1 Pet. 5:8-11)

We have an enemy, Satan, who wants to destroy our faith in Christ. He is described as one who is seeking to devour all believers. He is also called *"the accuser of our brethren, who accused them before our God day and night."* (Rev. 12:10)

Because we have such an enemy, we must learn to stand against him. How can we mortals stand against the power of the devil? The Bible says, *"By faith you stand!"* (2 Cor. 1:24). Romans 5:1-2 repeats the theme of standing by faith in the supplied grace of God: *"Therefore, having been justified by faith, we have peace with God through our Lord Jesus Christ, through whom also we have access by faith into this grace in which we stand, and rejoice in hope of the glory of God."*

This is powerful! What is coming to you and me from our Father is nothing less than what was being supplied to Jesus. However, our supply of grace has in it the victory over sin, death, demons, the world, the flesh, and yes, even the devil. We have within us Jesus Christ, victor over Satan, *"because as He is, so are we in this world."* (1 John 4:17) With all boldness and assurance of faith, let us stand fast in our endowment of grace. Because Jesus suffered the whole spectrum of challenges in victorious overcoming godliness, He has become the supplier of *"all grace"* to everyone who turns to Him. What are you facing humanly? Jesus is able to supply the kind of grace that is necessary to more than adequately meet that need and enable you to stand strong in the Lord.

In Philippians 1:27-28 Paul exhorts the saints,

> *"Only let your conduct be worthy of the gospel of Christ, so that whether I come and see you or am absent, I may hear of your affairs, that you stand fast in one spirit, with one mind striving together for the faith of the gospel, and not in any way terrified by your adversaries."*

This is how we resist the devil. We stand firm in the truth of what the Bible says. We do not deviate based on feeling or circumstance. We will have nothing to do with compromise or political correctness or any semblance of deceitfulness. We will not let the enemies of God weaken our faith because we know that our strength to stand comes from our Father in heaven.

Paul also gives us strong encouragement to stand by taking on the full armor of God because the matter of standing is primarily regarding the assaults of Satan our enemy.

> *"Finally, my brethren, be strong in the Lord and in the power of His might. Put on the whole armor of God, that you may be able to stand against the wiles of the devil. For we do not wrestle against flesh and blood, but against principalities, against powers, against the rulers of the darkness of this age, against spiritual hosts of wickedness in the heavenly places. Therefore take up the whole armor of God that you may be able to withstand in the evil day, and having done all, to stand.*
>
> *Stand therefore, having girded your waist with truth, having put on the breastplate of righteousness, and having shod your feet with the preparation of the gospel of peace; above all, taking the shield of faith with which you will be able to quench all the fiery darts of the wicked one. And take the helmet of salvation, and the sword of the Spirit, which [Spirit] is the word of God; praying always with all prayer and supplication in the Spirit, being watchful to this end with all perseverance and supplication for all the saints."*

(Eph. 6:10-18)

Doesn't this instill courage and boldness in us? If God is for us in this way, who or what can stand against us?

It is by the continuous supply of God's grace that we are enabled to stand. We must avoid being entangled again with the old covenant law.

> *"Stand fast therefore in the liberty by which Christ has made us free, and do not be entangled again with a yoke of bondage."*

(Gal. 5:1)

No strength is imparted through the law. We have already talked about how easy it is to fall from grace by trying to fulfill what we cannot. So let's stop dabbling around with anything related to the law. The law of God is good, but we are sold under sin and the flesh cannot ever fulfill the law. The law may seem good for a little while, but there is no saving virtue in it to make us stand before God and against our enemy.

Have you ever done something that you just did because somebody else said you needed to do it? But in your heart only mumbling and hostility seemed to exist. You went ahead and did what was expected of you, but your heart wasn't in it. You weren't proud of the work you did because your mind was mostly on trying to get it over with. That is so much like the demands of the law. The law cannot give life. But the Spirit of grace can give you life to do everything and do it with joy. The end result will be approved by God, and you will rejoice with Him. One who has learned this lesson of receiving grace supplied by God and letting God's supplied grace do the task at hand will be both established in grace and stand in grace against the evil one.

Hearing and knowing of the success of other believers helps us to stand fast in grace through all of our own circumstances. Paul tenderly tells the saints,

> *"Therefore, brethren, in all our affliction and distress we were comforted concerning you by your faith. For now we live, if you stand fast in the Lord. For what thanks can we render to God for you, for all the joy with which we rejoice for your sake before our God, night and day praying exceedingly that we may see your face and perfect what is lacking in your faith?"*

(1 Thess. 3:9-10)

Standing firm in the faith is also learning to rejoice in the triumphs of our fellow believers. As our Christian friends experience victory in Christ and tell us about it, we are encouraged and our faith increases.

> *"But we are bound to give thanks to God always for you, brethren beloved by the Lord, because God from the beginning chose you for salvation through sanctification by the Spirit and belief in the truth, to which He called you by our gospel, for the obtaining of the glory of our Lord Jesus Christ. Therefore, brethren, stand fast and hold the traditions which you were taught, whether by word or our epistle."*

(2 Thess. 2:13-15)

In these verses Paul is exhorting the brethren to stand fast in the traditions because some evil workers had come to distract the church from the simplicity that is in Christ. The saints in Thessalonica were standing firm in the Lord. This became their ability to stand in the face of satanic opposers and persecution. Their victory in this became a great comfort to Paul. The traditions were the things which pertain to Christ as their life. This was a part of the young church's warfare against deceivers.

There was a co-worker of Paul who is an outstanding example of standing in the grace which God was supplying. His name was Epaphras.

> *"Epaphras, who is one of you, a bondservant of Christ, greets you, always laboring fervently for you in prayers, that you may stand perfect and complete in all the will of God. For I bear him witness that he has a great zeal for you, and those who are in Laodicea, and those in Hierapolis."*

(Col. 4:12-13)

This should be the description of everyone that is standing in the grace which God has supplied. Christ has destroyed the works of the devil, *"having disarmed principalities and powers, He made a public spectacle of them, triumphing over them in it"* (Col. 2:15). That is the gospel we have heard, believed and are standing in.

To stand in the grace of God against the wiles of the devil has practical ramifications. In the church in Corinth a brother had committed a sin of fornication with his father's wife. The whole church was rebuked by Paul for not dealing with the sinful brother. The apostle sternly told them to cast the sinful man out of the congregation. After some time the sinful brother mournfully repented of the sin he had committed. When

Paul heard of the brother's repentance, he urged the church to forgive the man and receive him back into the fellowship.

> *"But if anyone has caused grief, he has not grieved me, but all of you to some extent — not to be too severe. This punishment which was inflicted by the majority is sufficient for such a man, so that, on the contrary, you ought rather to forgive and comfort him, lest perhaps such a one be swallowed up with too much sorrow. Therefore I urge you to reaffirm your love to him. For to this end I also wrote that I might put you to the test, whether you are obedient in all things. Now whom you forgive anything, I also forgive. For if indeed I have forgiven anything, I have forgiven that one for your sakes in the presence of Christ, lest Satan should take advantage of us; for we are not ignorant of his devices."*

(2 Cor. 2:5-11)

This is one of the profound revelations of the New Testament experience and ministry of grace. Paul was doing what he did in the person of Christ. The word in Greek that is translated *"presence"* is "prospone." It literally means in the face around the eyes. Paul did his forgiving act by looking into the eyes of Jesus. Paul was standing in the grace of God in both rebuking and forgiving because he was fighting against Satan, not the sinful person whom God loved. This is how we too are to reign in life through the One—Jesus Christ! And notice that the forgiven brother was helped to stand in order that he might not be overtaken by extreme sorrow.

Grace is supplied and is available for every human circumstance. It is the sphere of God in which we are called to live. Therefore we are to grow in this grace continually. Grace is also the divine life flowing from God by which we are established in the victory of Christ. Grace is God Himself flowing to us through the bountiful supply of the Holy Spirit to overcome Satan. By grace our Father supplies and sustains us in every conceivable human eventuality. Take grace now—lay hold of it—it is yours!

CONCLUDING THOUGHTS

Indeed grace flows like a river from God our Father and the Lord Jesus Christ. It at times flows like a gentle stream. At other times it is like the Mississippi growing to overwhelming proportions as it flows, drawing its volume from its numerous tributaries. Our experience of the grace from our loving Father is predestined to be like this. How is it flowing in you? Again I mention these two inviting words I learned from the Lord—receive and let. That is our rapturous part in this journey into God.

The more I read the verses in God's Word revealing His grace, the more I am filled with inward awe, expectation, and satisfaction regarding my salvation. At times I am speechless before Him. In those holy moments, I can only lift my head and hands in worship and wipe the tears of joy and thankfulness from my eyes. It is as though I am transported into the very presence of Abba, and there I am embraced by all the wonder of His unspeakable Gift—Jesus. There while being held in Abba's arms, He opens yet more vistas of His grace and purpose according to the *"good pleasure of His will"* for me.

To the principalities and powers in the universe, our Father wants to display us as the consummate evidence of His love and wisdom. It is Abba's purpose from the beginning

> *"...to make all see what is the fellowship of the mystery, which from the beginning of the ages has been hidden in God who created all things through Jesus Christ; to the intent that now the manifold wisdom of God might be made known by the church to the principalities and powers in the heavenly places, according to the eternal purpose which He accomplished in Christ Jesus our Lord, in whom we have boldness and access with confidence through faith in Him."*

(Eph. 3:9-12)

Today and for the rest of our days, Abba wants to unfold to us the wonders of His grace that is now within us and also that which is to be brought to us at the revelation of our Lord and Savior, Jesus Christ. It is expedient that you and I sink deeply and thoroughly into this abundantly supplied grace. Great grace is upon us all. Now to you, dear reader, the Lord inquires as in John 14:9:

> *"Have I been with you so long, and yet you have not known Me...?"*

He awaits your response!